THE
ULTIMATE
WOOD
FIRED
OVEN
COOKBOOK

GENEVIEVE TAYLOR

Hardie Grant

QUADRILLE

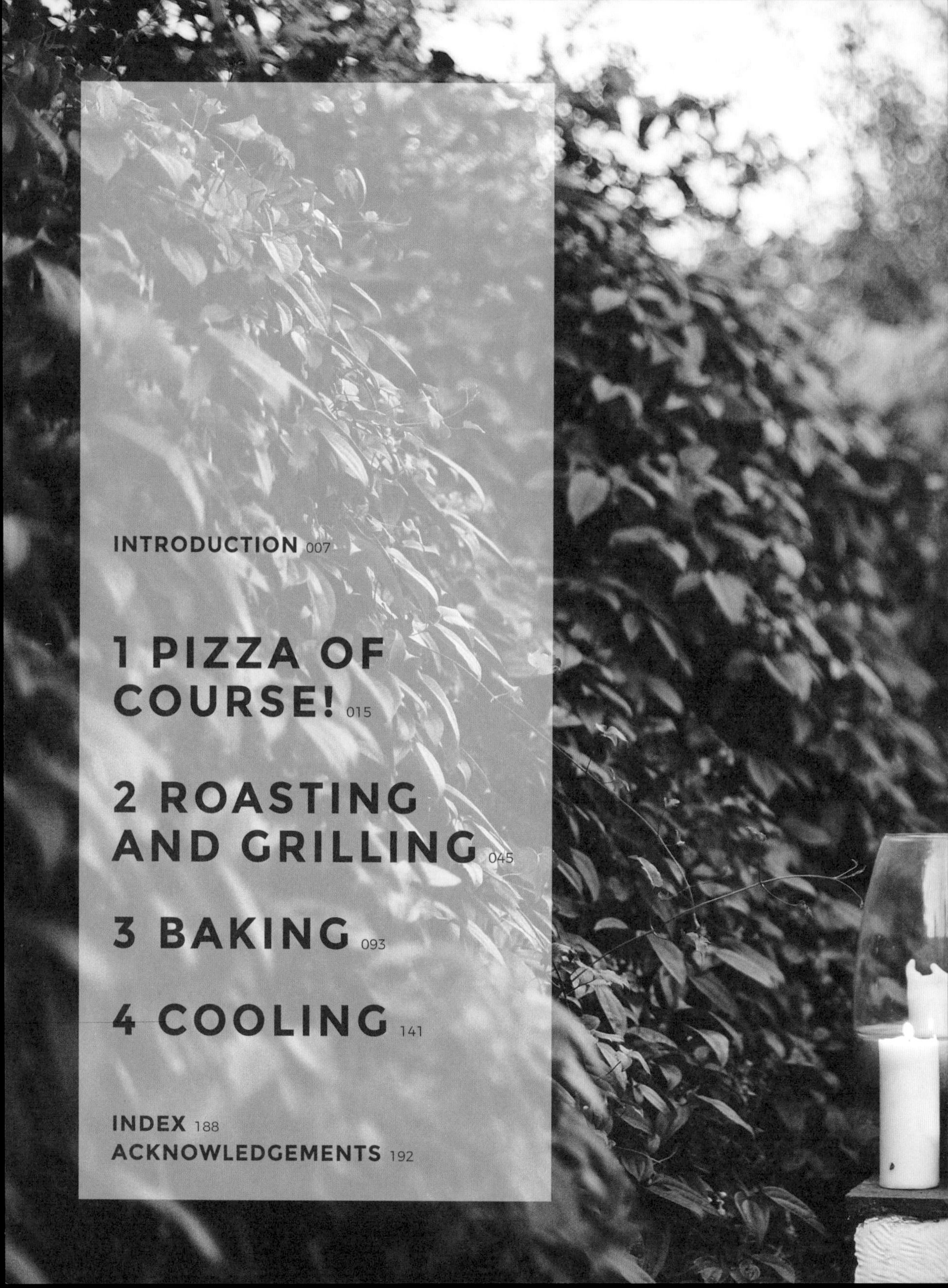

INTRODUCTION

Cooking with wood is wonderfully addictive, and I hope this book will inspire you to get outside and make the most of your wood-fired oven.

Owning a wood-fired oven has become so desirable in recent years, but why bother when you have a perfectly good oven in your kitchen? For me, it's about throwing off the shackles of technology, embracing a bit of culinary adventure and getting back to basics with that most primal of elements, fire. The sense of achievement you feel from striking a single match and mastering a fire in which you can cook a multitude of dishes is, quite simply, huge.

If there is one thing I want to shout from the rooftops, it is that the oven you bought to make perfect wood-fired pizza will also make a million and one other things just as brilliantly. The breadth of dishes you can get out of a wood-fired oven is almost limitless – you can roast, grill, barbecue and smoke in it, as well as use it as a hob and a giant slow cooker. Within these pages you will find not only a multitude of pizza ideas but delicious breads, cakes and puddings, alongside inspiration for kebabs, quick roasts and slow braises from all over the world. There is even a marmalade mousse, a wood-fired cream tea, an overnight fruit cake for Christmas and a pot of steaming porridge for breakfast. Your wood-fired oven is a tremendously versatile cooking tool, ripe and ready for exploration.

Without temperature dials and fan controls you become a more intuitive cook, one who values their senses of smell, sight, taste and even touch over the beep of the oven timer. You will need to free yourself from the idea of set recipe times and cooking temperatures – as a professional recipe writer this has been both challenging and liberating. So, while the recipes within these pages do come with times and temperatures, I would urge you not to be bound by them; more important is cultivating an attitude of 'it's done when it's done', and a willingness to work in tandem with your fire. Like mastering anything new, practice and repetition build confidence, and with confidence comes success. You will have times when the oven doesn't perform as you want it to – I still get the odd day like that if it's particularly damp or cold – but persist and you will reap the rewards.

Cooking in a wood-fired oven is hugely sociable, so don't be surprised if friends and neighbours gather round your fire and want to get involved. It's also worth saying that I really hope you use your oven year round, not just on balmy summer evenings. These ovens are a real investment, both in time and money, whichever sort you have, so it's great to make the most of them.

The most satisfying part of wood-fired cookery is learning how to maximize the gently falling curve of temperature to cook multiple dishes. The recipes in this book reduce in temperature the further you delve through, the idea being that you start with the hottest things and move through to the coolest. Once you have generated a good fire with expensive kiln-dried wood, it absolutely pays to have several dishes prepped that you can add in, one after the other, as your oven cools down. This means that you can get several meals ready for future eating; stews and soups are great for this, as well as breads and cakes. There is tremendous satisfaction from knowing you are squeezing every drop of energy out of your fire.

I can be found on social media as @genevieveeats, so do wave hello, hit me with your wood-fired questions and share pictures of your ovens and edible creations!

WHAT SORT OF OVEN TO CHOOSE?

There are loads of different wood-fired ovens out there, from fixed ovens like mine made of brick and stone, to rather dinky table-top and portable ovens, and if you are yet to buy your oven there are lots of things to think about to help you choose which is right for you. Here are some points to consider:

• How much room do you have? Can the oven be fixed in place, or do you need to move it around your garden or store it inside for the winter if it's not weatherproof?
• Portable ovens, like the Uuni or Roccbox, are brilliant for a sleek, compact design and a relatively affordable price tag. And if you move house you can take it with you.
• Metal ovens heat up faster and therefore you can cook on them sooner, but they also tend to cool down more quickly, which can limit the range of food you can cook.
• Built-in brick or stone ovens have more potential for insulation. If you want to cook using retained heat for several hours, or even overnight, you will need an oven that's well insulated on the top, bottom and sides. Wanting to maximize the full range of cooking options available, this is the oven I chose, but it's a serious investment in terms of both money and garden space.
• Big isn't necessarily best – bigger ovens do take longer to heat up – and if pizza is your primary aim, bear in mind they only take a couple of minutes to cook so you don't necessarily need to fit several in at once (and it's often easier to cook singly anyway; see the pizza chapter, page 15, for pizza-making tips). But bigger ovens also take longer to cool, so can be excellent if you are keen on low and slow cooking. I found a middle-sized oven offered the best of both worlds for what I wanted.

MY OVEN

All the recipes in this book were tested in a wood-fired oven in my back garden in Bristol. I cook in a medium-sized, well-insulated dome oven which I bought as a kit from Gozney Ovens, a Dorset-based company which designs and manufactures them locally. The oven itself is DEFRA approved for use in smoke-controlled areas, important as I live in a smoke-controlled city and wanted to make sure my oven was as energy-efficient as possible. I burn only very low moisture content, kiln-dried timber and compressed sawdust bricks, not only for their superior cooking heat but also because of the lower smoke and particulate emissions that come from a more efficient burn. The oven is supremely well insulated top and bottom, and with one really good fire I can be

cooking in it for 24 hours, or even a little more, as the heat falls gently away over time.

My husband and I installed it ourselves, a physically hard but rewarding job that took several weekends of very hard graft. We started by building a solid base with good foundations that acts as a log and tool store underneath the oven, on which sit layers of insulating board atop a grid of strong concrete lintels. The dome itself was positioned on top, offset from the centre to give me a wide shelf for food preparation, and then insulated with thick thermal wool before adding a 10cm (4in) thick coat of vermiculite-concrete mix skimmed over with a flexible render. All in all it's a very sturdy beast indeed and it's going nowhere. We filmed the build process in time-lapse, and you can find the film on my YouTube channel should you wish to see it in more detail (search for GenevieveEatsTV).

WHERE TO PUT YOUR OVEN?

Site your oven somewhere close to the house if possible, with the possibility for a shelter over it to protect it (and you!) from the elements should the weather turn inclement. This can be a permanent shed roof if you have space and don't mind the restricted view it might create, or something movable like a garden parasol – just be sure to keep it well away from the oven flue. I use a canvas parasol because I know my oven itself is very well protected from the elements and it's only the cook that might need a little shelter from time to time.

If you are building your oven, the more room around the oven you can create, either with a built-in worktop or an outside table, the more practical it will be for cooking in – just like in an inside kitchen, there is little more frustrating to a keen cook than a lack of worktop space. Ideally you would store your tools and wood underneath your oven so you can just grab as necessary – another pro-point for building your own if you can. It's great to be able to design it so it works 'just so'.

LIGHTING AND MANAGING THE FIRE

For me, lighting the fire is a really joyful bit of the wood-fired cooking process. I enjoy it immensely, and like most passionate 'fire-starters' I have my own very particular way of doing it. The way I was taught to light a fire – I can't remember now by whom or when: my dad? My big brother? The cubs? – was that you start small and build up, gradually adding bigger and bigger bits of fuel to a base of a firelighter and kindling. Certainly this is a tried and tested route, known as the bottom-up method, and it works very well, but it can be somewhat high-maintenance.

More recently I have become an almost evangelical convert to the total opposite way, the top-down method. For this you build a neat Jenga stack of logs on a metal peel, starting with a row of the biggest along the bottom and building up to a bundle of kindling on top. On top of that I place a natural firelighter, a wax-dipped ball of wood shavings, and I strike a match. Once the firelighter has caught well, I slide the peel into the centre of the oven and carefully push the stack off the peel on to the oven floor so it stays neatly stacked. The firelighter lights the kindling underneath it, which in turn drops embers on to the next layer of small logs, which then ignites and drops embers on to the layer below, until you end up with a roaring fire. The great benefit of this is that you strike the match, watch for a minute or so to make sure the kindling is catching, then walk away until the oven is super-hot – in my case about an hour later. Two potential stumbling blocks with this method – if your oven is small and portable and you can't fit a whole fire's worth of fuel in at once, or if the doorway is too low.

Experiment with your fires, light them often and learn as you go along, finding out what you like and what works best in your own oven.

OPTIMUM OVEN FIRING

In most cases it's best to fire up your oven to an optimum temperature and then let it cool down, using that falling curve of the heat to cook multiple dishes one after the other. An oven that has its walls, base and roof saturated and soaked with heat energy becomes a much more stable chamber to cook in. This is especially important for baking, as an even heat is desirable over an oven with hot and cool spots.

Once your oven is fired up to optimum temperature you will notice the dark soot clearing from the roof, leaving a small white spot that extends and spreads over the roof. However, you can use the increasing heat of a growing fire to quickly roast things like vegetables for topping pizzas, without having to wait for this to happen.

FUEL

You will always be disappointed by your oven's heat output if you try to burn damp fuel – it will smoke too much and be generally very frustrating. Use the best quality kiln-dried wood you can, and it will pay you back handsomely in fuel efficiency and food output. I also use compressed sawdust bricks, an eco-friendly by-product of the timber industry, as they burn very hot and cleanly with practically no ash to speak of. I find a combination of both of these works best for my oven. You can also dry out regular bags of seasoned logs in a cooling oven overnight (provided there are no embers that could set them alight), something I don't often do, as I'd rather use the oven as a slow cooker for getting the next day's meals together. I always start my fire with a single, natural firelighter, a very neat little bundle of wood shavings dipped in wax that doesn't give off nasty fumes like regular firelighters.

MEASURING THE TEMPERATURE

It's actually more tricky than you might think to accurately measure the temperature of your oven, another very good reason to free your mind from the idea of rigid cooking temperatures. I cannot tell you to 'bung it in the oven at 180°C (350°F) for 20 minutes' with any degree of confidence that it will come out cooked properly. The reasons for this are multi-layered – where you take your temperature will differ from where I took mine, an infra-red thermometer (see Essential equipment, page 12) will only give you a reading for a specific point on the floor, it will tell you neither the air temperature nor the rate at which the heat of the oven is rising or falling. A built-in door thermometer is a pretty reliable way of measuring the oven's air temperature, but if you have the door on and off frequently that won't work very accurately, and if you are cooking with live flames you can't put the door on or you will starve the fire of oxygen.

As a general rule, you add food when the oven is a little hotter than you might expect, as when you add it, it will absorb energy and reduce the overall temperature. Remember that by lighting a fire you have given your oven a source of energy, created a battery of energy if you like, and that by adding food you are draining the power from that battery. It stands to reason that a heavy-duty cast-iron casserole that is full of cold liquid and a joint of dense, uncooked meat will suck out way more energy than a thin metal plate with a single fillet of fish on it. Cooking several things at once is a great way to maximize cooking output if your oven is big enough, but by adding more you will find the temperature falls quicker than if you just had a single dish in the oven. This battery analogy is the main reason a well-insulated oven is the best option for cooking the widest range of dishes; more insulation simply equals a bigger store of energy available for cooking.

CONTROLLING THE TEMPERATURE

You will need to learn how to increase and decrease the temperature of your oven; it's a vital skill for wood-fired oven success. A lot of the recipes in this book have a flexible temperature range, and I have tried to make it clear which ones these are, meaning you can simply cook them hotter or cooler, they will just take less or more time accordingly.

You can increase the heat by adding more fuel, so have a good supply of wrist-thick logs handy so you can add them one at a time to keep the fire stoked. Logs that are too large won't catch fire quickly and may cause excess smoking. Provided your fuel is good and dry, it's possible to add a little fuel while you have food in the oven, as it will catch quickly and easily, but if your fire is having a sulk it's often better to get all the food out, stoke it up with plenty of fuel and get it going with a good puff on the invaluable copper pipe (see Essential equipment, overleaf). Once your fire is lit and you know you are going to want it to stay at a good temperature for a while, it's best to regularly add small logs to keep it burning well. There is a point in every fire's life that, once passed, means it's hard to get it going again easily. If you find you get to this point with your fire, better to admit defeat, pull out the food, then relight the fire properly using another firelighter and some kindling if necessary.

You can also increase the heat available for cooking by using the metal peel to move your fire around the oven, thus revealing a hot spot where the fire was. The area underneath the fire will be really hot, and this could be the heat boost your dish needs to finish it off properly. My fire can often sulk a bit if I move it from one side of the oven to the other, so I reach once again for the copper pipe to give it a little blow and get it going again. Regularly moving the fire from one side to the other is a good habit to get into, as it means the oven develops an even heat all over, thus becoming more stable.

To decrease the heat you can stop adding fuel so it reduces in temperature naturally, a process that can be quick if there's little insulation and often frustratingly slow if there is a lot of insulation. You can also leave the door off, again a slow process if your oven is well insulated. To cool my oven quite quickly I shove in a large stockpot full of cold water, which absorbs the energy and gets up to boiling point surprisingly fast.

As a bonus, you can then pour it into the sink to do the washing-up. Never be tempted to throw water directly on to the oven floor, as you can crack it.

WORKING WITH A DAMP, COLD OVEN

It's worth noting that an oven that is used regularly will always outperform one that only gets fired up once a month. My oven has a proper sulk if it's it been out of action for any length of time, and if I know I need it to fire perfectly on any given day (for a party, for instance), I will make sure I light it the day before to start getting it warmed up. If your oven hasn't been used for ages and is very damp and cold, it's often a good idea to light a series of little 'pulse fires' to gently bring it up in temperature slowly. A quickly raging fire in a stone-cold oven has the potential to lead to cracks developing in the dome.

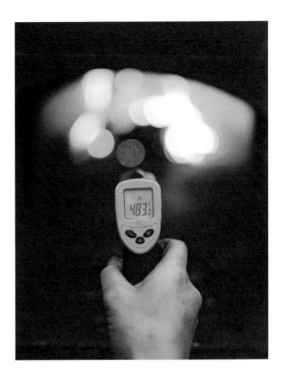

ESSENTIAL EQUIPMENT

With all that good dry fuel, you are going to need a few bits of specialist equipment that can deal with the extreme temperatures inside your oven.

Welders' gauntlets

I'm afraid regular oven gloves don't really cut it for wood-fired cooking. Thick leather welders' gauntlets that come well up your forearms offer ideal protection, although it's slightly frustrating that they usually come in a standard size of 'massive'. Manufacturers take note: girls rather like fires too.

Infra-red thermometer

An infra-red thermometer is invaluable for gauging a picture of the heat inside your oven, by scanning it across the floor and walls to give an idea of hot and cool spots. Be sure to buy one that goes up to 500°C (930°F) plus – some max out around 300–350°C (570–660°F), which just isn't high enough for a wood-fired oven.

A wooden peel

A wooden peel is used for making pizzas on and sliding them into the oven. Wood is the best choice for raw dough – it's way more insulating than metal, so there is much less chance of the dough sticking as you manoeuvre the pizza into place. It's also good for sliding bread into the oven to cook.

A metal peel

A metal peel is better for turning and removing pizza and loaves, as it has a much slimmer profile, enabling it to slide easily between oven floor and food. It's also quite a good choice for rotating lighter dishes and pans, although it will struggle with heavy cast iron. I always build my fire on my metal peel at the entrance to the oven before sliding it into the centre, and I also use it for moving the fire around the oven once lit.

A hook on a pole

A long pole with a hook on the end is really useful for dragging roasting tins and heavy pots and pans out the oven, and also for prodding the logs about a bit. You can buy special coal hooks for this purpose, but mine is a little more makeshift – a brass hook that is meant for opening and shutting sash windows, fixed to the end of a slightly cut-down broom handle.

A length of copper pipe

Cooking directly on the oven floor is known as 'bare baking', and a long length of copper pipe is invaluable for puffing away ash from the oven floor before you cook directly on it. Use a hammer to slightly squish the end nearest the fire for a more directional blow. It's also great for giving the fire a little boost of air to get it going. All in all one of my favourite, and most simple, tools for the wood-fired oven. A fan is also good for swooshing a bit of air on to a sulky fire – I have a wicker one I picked up for a euro in a Portuguese supermarket, worth every cent.

Cooking trays, pots and pans

Most cooking equipment you have for your kitchen can be used in your oven, just as long as there are no plastic or wooden handles. I shove my regular roasting tins and saucepans in without a worry – the thinner ones may warp a little at extreme temperatures, but they generally spring back again once cold. Cheap and cheerful metal plates and platters, the kind you might find in an Indian restaurant, are good, as they conduct heat super-fast and therefore are great for flash-roasting or searing, or for resting whole veg for overnight roasting, or for quickly toasting spices in a coolish oven. They may also discolour, bend and warp a little, but no matter. For slow cooking, stoneware and terracotta are excellent choices.

Cast iron is a fabulous choice for slow braising and casseroles. It can crack under extreme temperatures, so I wouldn't rest it directly over embers or shove it right into the intense heat of a raging fire, but for general roasting, baking and slow cooking under 300°C (570°F), it's fine. Heavy-duty steel is another brilliant choice, as it's virtually indestructible. You do need to keep steel pots and pans well seasoned to protect them from rust. After use, wash gently – no fierce scouring – and dry well, then wipe over with a little vegetable oil and set over a high heat (or shove into your hot oven) to 'set' the oil into a really thin, naturally non-stick layer.

If you want to turn your wood-fired oven into a barbecue, you need a grill. You can buy special grills, but I improvise with an upturned 'fish cage' meant for the barbecue.

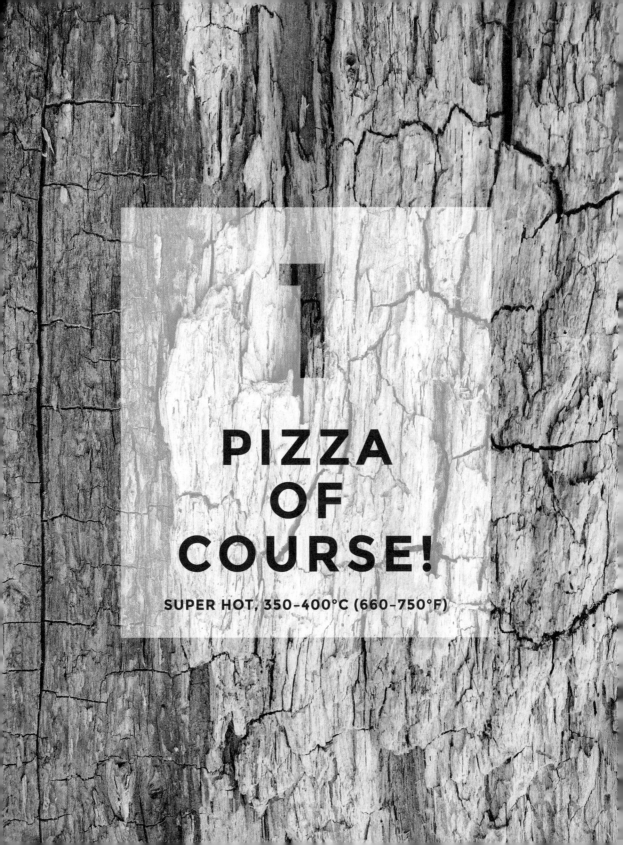

PIZZA
OF
COURSE!

SUPER HOT, 350–400°C (660–750°F)

The allure of pizza is something most of us can relate to. Dreams of wood-fired pizza were certainly the reason I first started fantasizing about owning a wood-fired oven, and I'd be willing to wager a bet that I'm far from alone. You simply cannot get a better pizza than one made in a wood oven and I hope this chapter will guide you through the process of achieving your desires with ease.

There is a single physical reason why wood-fired pizzas are far superior to oven-baked ones, and that is heat. A domestic oven is capable of getting to something like 220–230°C (425–450°F), while with a well-constructed, well-insulated wood-fired oven it's entirely possible to achieve temperatures of over double that. Often my wood oven is way too hot for pizza, getting up to 500°C (930°F) or even higher, and I need to wait for it to settle down to an ideal pizza temperature, which is about 350–400°C (660–750°F).

A hotter oven leads to a more rapid 'oven spring', the baker's term for the rising and setting of the dough. With more heat, the air trapped inside the bubbles of your dough expands and rises quicker, the result being a lighter, airier pizza base. You also get a greater contrast of textures between a crisp, lightly charred outside and a soft, puffy, fluffy interior. Never underestimate the power of texture when it comes to food – pair something crispy and crunchy with something soft and melty (sounds like a perfect pizza, right?) and you are heading towards food nirvana.

Great pizza is not just about the base, although that's a pretty critical starting point – it's also about what you put on top. I think the reason pizzas are such great party food is simply that they can be made as individual as you are. Like going to a dinner party with an à la carte menu, you get to decide what's on and what's not on your own pizza. There are a few 'rules' when it comes to toppings – the key one is: don't overdo it. Less is definitely more with pizza. It's better to choose a few things that are intensely flavoured rather than a lot of toppings that are watery and bland.

While pizza perfection is entirely achievable, it does take a little practice to get right, and you may have a few misshapen, wonky attempts as you are climbing up the learning curve. They will still taste pretty fine, so eat up and move on to the next time. With each firing of your oven, with every pizza you shape and top, I guarantee you will get better and better.

A PIZZA TIMELINE!

I am not normally a fan of military-style operations when it comes to cooking, but I'm afraid with pizza you have little option but to be brutally organized. Wood-fired pizzas cook quickly, exceedingly quickly, and if your oven is running to optimum temperature you can expect each pizza to cook in just a couple of minutes. This is both a blessing and something of a curse. The intense heat from the fire will cook the best pizza you have ever tasted, but the transition from perfection to burnt is rather a rapid one. Therefore you need to be ready and armed, with all the steps thought through and covered before you begin.

With that in mind, here is an at-a-glance timeline of the things you need to think about. All the steps below are sequentially covered in much more detail on the following pages.

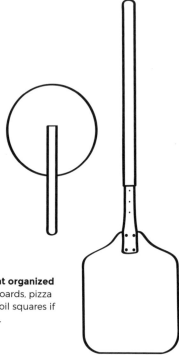

3 **Get your equipment organized** – peels, chopping boards, pizza wheels or scissors, foil squares if you are using them.

1 **Start your dough**, a good 2–3 hours before you want to cook your first pizza.

2 Once the dough is having its initial prove, make the base sauce – either one of the traditional tomato sauces (see page 21), or try the white pizza sauce (see page 21) for something deliciously different.

4 **Shape the dough into balls** and rest them on well-floured baking sheets – they need a second prove of an hour or so before turning them into thin, round pizzas.

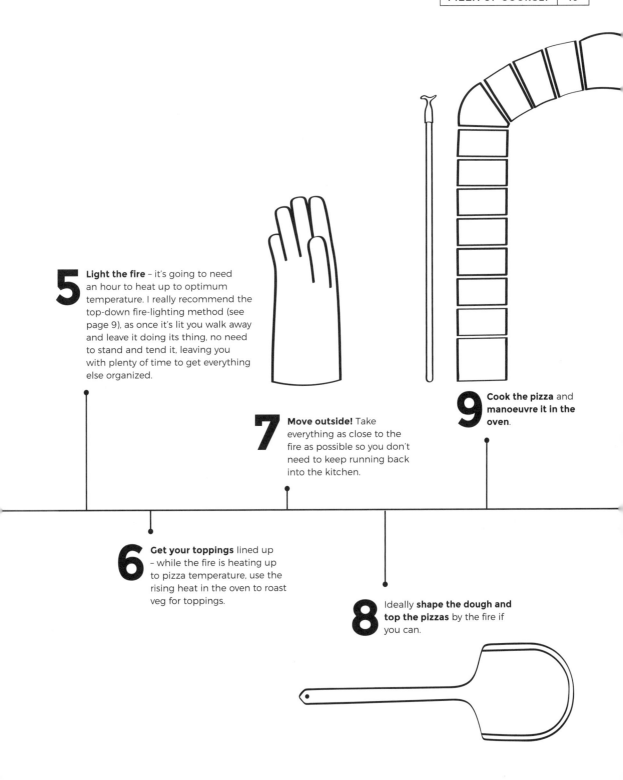

5 **Light the fire** – it's going to need an hour to heat up to optimum temperature. I really recommend the top-down fire-lighting method (see page 9), as once it's lit you walk away and leave it doing its thing, no need to stand and tend it, leaving you with plenty of time to get everything else organized.

7 **Move outside!** Take everything as close to the fire as possible so you don't need to keep running back into the kitchen.

9 **Cook the pizza** and **manoeuvre it in the oven**.

6 **Get your toppings** lined up – while the fire is heating up to pizza temperature, use the rising heat in the oven to roast veg for toppings.

8 Ideally **shape the dough and top the pizzas** by the fire if you can.

THE PIZZA BASE
– PERFECT DOUGH

Memorable pizza may be about the flavours you put on top, but you can't have a great pizza with an inferior base. Perhaps boringly but very unashamedly, I like to keep my bases pretty traditional with a simple, olive-oil-enriched dough. Perfect pizza is a thin, well-baked crust with a slightly thicker rim that's airy and puffed up. For me this is not the time to experiment with unusual flours and techniques in the way I might with other bread doughs. So I have given one recipe alone for a pizza base, but it is rather a good one . . .

Flour and yeast

I use regular strong white bread flour for my pizza dough. It's something I always have in my cupboard, it's very easy to buy and it's cheap. Some baking aficionados may insist upon a super-fine milled '00' Italian flour, and while this is great and worth experimenting with if you have some, I have found regular strong white bread flour to yield very good results.

With regards to yeast I always use Doves Farm 'quick yeast', which you can find really easily in most large supermarkets, but any instant, fast-acting yeast is fine. At the risk of sounding like an appalling name-dropper, I was working with Paul Hollywood a few years ago, baking him a loaf with regular dried yeast, and he told me quite sternly that he always uses instant yeast, no need to rehydrate with warm water and sugar before you start. Well, if it's good enough for Paul . . .

If you have a sourdough starter, feel free to use this in place of yeast to get your dough fermenting. I would replace the yeast with about 200g (7oz) of starter per batch of the recipe below, reducing the flour to 800g (6 cups) and adding as much water as you need to get a soft dough. You will know the strength of your starter and may need to adjust these rough guidelines accordingly. My advice would be to follow the recipe here a few times to get a feel for the right consistency, then aim to replicate that with the water, flour and sourdough starter ratios in a sourdough mix.

LOW-KNEAD PIZZA DOUGH

This is the pizza dough I have come to swear by, and it's based on a recipe from Dan Lepard's excellent baking book, Short and Sweet. It's the easiest recipe ever, requiring practically no kneading, just a few gentle pushes and pulls of the dough on an oiled worktop, which feels heavenly, like squishing a super-soft, warm feather pillow. In fact, most of the bread I ever make now follows Dan's minimal knead method.

The second prove, after shaping the dough into balls, is essential to allow the gluten to relax, meaning you can gently flatten the dough balls into large thin bases without the dough springing back on itself.

THIS RECIPE MAKES ENOUGH DOUGH FOR 8 LARGE PIZZAS – simply halve it if you are feeding fewer people. If you are feeding more, make separate batches in two bowls, otherwise it will be too unwieldy.

900g (6½ cups) strong white bread flour, plus more for shaping and stretching the dough
2 tsp fast-action yeast
2 tsp fine salt
600ml (2½ cups) hand-hot water
4 tbsp olive oil, plus more for working the dough

Put the flour, yeast and salt into a mixing bowl and stir together. Pour in the water and oil, mixing until you have a shaggy mass with no loose flour. Cover with a clean tea towel and leave to stand for 10 minutes.

Lightly oil a good-sized patch of worktop and rub a little oil on to your hands. Scrape the dough out on to the worktop, then scrape any loose bits out of the bowl and rub a little oil around the inside, setting it aside ready for the dough to go back in.

Very lightly knead the dough for just 10 seconds – one gentle push-and-pull is 1 second. Treat the dough with kid gloves, you don't need to pummel it. Lift the dough into the oiled bowl, re-cover and leave for 10 more minutes. Repeat the gentle 10-second knead with a 10-minute rest two more times, then cover and leave until risen by 50 per cent. This will take an hour or so, depending on the room temperature. If you want to leave it longer, it will happily sit in the fridge for 4–6 hours. Remove from the fridge an hour before you want to shape it, so it comes up to room temperature.

Now you can move on to making sauces and organizing your equipment.

THREE PIZZA SAUCES...

I have two tomato sauces I turn to for pizza: the first is a store-cupboard version using a carton of passata, and the second is made by roasting fresh tomatoes in the oven. The latter gives a much paler sauce, but what it lacks in colour it certainly makes up for in flavour (although I would only consider making it when tomatoes are cheap and plentiful). Both sauces need to be cool before you use them, so I generally make them while the dough is proving, or even on an entirely separate day. They will keep in the fridge for 4–5 days or in the freezer for 3 months. At a pinch you could just use a drizzle of passata straight from the carton if you were pushed for time, but do add a little salt and pepper to it.

Both tomato sauce recipes make enough for 8 large pizzas – you only need a tablespoon or so for each pizza.

STORE-CUPBOARD TOMATO SAUCE

500g (2¼ cups) passata
1 clove of garlic, crushed
a pinch of dried oregano
1 tbsp olive oil
1 tsp granulated sugar
salt and freshly ground black pepper

Put everything into a small heavy-based saucepan and bring to the boil on the hob. Turn the heat down to a steady simmer and allow to putter away for a good 20 minutes, until thick and rich. Tip into a bowl and set aside to cool completely before using on your pizzas.

FRESH ROAST TOMATO SAUCE

200–220°C (400–425°F)

750g (1lb 10oz) ripe tomatoes, chopped
3 cloves of garlic, peeled and left whole
3 tbsp olive oil
a few sprigs of fresh oregano or marjoram, leaves picked (or 1 tsp of dried)
salt and freshly ground black pepper

You need your oven at a good roasting temperature (200–220°C/400–425°F) for this recipe. You can use your wood oven as it's coming up to pizza temperature, or

'cheat' and make it in your kitchen oven if you have other veg in the wood oven.

Put the tomatoes into a deep roasting tin so they fit in a snug layer – you don't want them too spaced out as they will colour too much. Add the garlic, drizzle over the oil, sprinkle over the herbs and season with salt and pepper.

Slide into the hot oven and roast for 30–40 minutes, stirring a couple of times during cooking so they cook evenly. If they are colouring too much, move them to a cooler part of the oven, or simply cook them for a little less time. Ideally you want them to collapse down, colour a little, and the juices to thicken and concentrate.

Once cooked, scrape the tomatoes into a food processor and purée until smooth, then spoon into a bowl and leave to cool completely before using. If you are making ahead of time, chill until needed. If you are in a hurry and want to make pizza with it straight away, pour it into a wide, shallow bowl to speed up cooling.

AND A WHITE PIZZA SAUCE

If tomato sauces are not your thing, or you just fancy ringing the changes, try this very easy, creamy, garlicky white pizza sauce. I really love it, and it's particularly good with seafood or salty vinegary capers. If you have any roast garlic left over (see page 37), you can use that in place of the raw garlic – just add to taste.

**MAKES ENOUGH FOR ABOUT 4 PIZZAS
(DOUBLE UP IF YOU WANT)**

250g (1¼ cups) mascarpone
25g (¼ cup) Parmesan, grated
1 clove of garlic, crushed
salt and freshly ground black pepper

Simply stir everything together in a bowl, adding 2–3 tablespoons of hot water from the kettle to thin the sauce to an easy spreading consistency.

BACK TO THE DOUGH – THE VITAL SECOND PROVE

A good hour before you want to cook your pizza, you need to shape the dough into balls, which I do just before lighting my fire. I know it takes a generous hour for my fire to come up to super-hot pizza temperature, conveniently about the same time the dough needs for a second prove. Your oven may take less or longer to heat, so adjust your timings accordingly – see below and the main introduction for fire advice.

Uncover the bowl of dough. Shake plenty of flour over the worktop, a little over your hands and over a sharp knife or dough cutter. Also shake plenty of flour over two large baking sheets and have these handy to put the balls of dough on. Ease the dough from the bowl on to the worktop using floured hands, taking care not to knock out all the bubbles – you just want to slide it out so the top still stays on the top. Gently pat it into an oblong and cut it in half, then pat each half back into an oblong again and cut those in half. Do this once more with each piece so you are left with 8 evenly sized pieces, all the time being gentle with the dough and patting it into shape rather than kneading, pulling or turning over.

Take a piece of dough and cup it between floured palms, rotating and gently pulling downwards as you turn the ball, teasing the edges underneath to give you a compact, tight ball shape with no folds or lines. Sprinkle a little flour over the ball and set on the floured baking sheet, then continue with the other 7 pieces of dough, spreading them out over two sheets so they don't stick together as they rise.

Set the dough balls to one side to prove for an hour or so while you fire up your oven. If you want to get ahead of the game, put the trays into the fridge, where they will sit happily for a few hours (but will take up quite a bit of room). If you refrigerate your dough balls, you need to take them out for 45 minutes or so to allow them to come up to room temperature before you try to stretch them out into pizzas. Cold dough doesn't behave very well, it is not very elastic and will have a tendency to spring back rather than stretch out.

PIZZA-MAKING EQUIPMENT

As well as the general wood fire equipment on page 12, there are some specific pizza-related tools you are going to need handy by the fire:

- A wooden peel for assembling and loading the uncooked pizza into the oven.
- A metal peel for taking the pizza out.
- Chopping boards or baking trays for transferring the cooked pizzas from the fire into the house or on to an outside table, wherever you are planning to eat.
- Something to cut your pizza up with – a pizza wheel is the obvious choice, but I find snipping through with a sharp pair of kitchen scissors much more efficient.
- If you are bare-baking your pizza directly on the oven floor, a copper blowpipe is the best tool for gently cleaning the ash off the floor before you slide the pizza on to it (see page 12).

LIGHTING A PIZZA FIRE

Once your dough is shaped up and is proving once more, it's time to get outside and light the fire. This is the bit I've come to love most; once you master lighting and working with fire it can be really rather addictive. Firelighting is covered a lot in the main introduction, but as an intense heat is absolutely critical to pizza success, it's worth reiterating a few points here:

• The **ideal pizza temperature** is in the rather dizzying range of 350–400°C (660–750°F), hugely hotter than a domestic oven. Use your infra-red thermometer to frequently monitor the base and roof heat of the oven and be prepared to wait until it's hot enough – there is no point attempting to cook a pizza until the oven is good and ready.

• You need to **get to know your oven**, as it will be different from mine – take the time to learn how it responds to heat, what it's like when you haven't used it for ages and it may be damp and cold (mine can be rather sulky). This is just a matter of using it as often as you can and being prepared to learn from failures, as well as making note of what you got right when your results are spot on.

• I always start with a **top-down fire** (see page 9) and I would really recommend you learn to love it too. One firelighter, one match, and you can walk away from the fire for an hour while it does its own thing. So simple, no tending and prodding and having to add incrementally larger fuel.

• You need a **strong bottom heat** to crisp the base quickly – so use the metal peel to move the fire around the oven a few times to make sure the base stones have really absorbed the energy from the fire.

• And you need a **strong radiant top heat** to melt the cheese and crisp up the crust – so make sure your initial fire was big enough to get a raging flame that rolled all around the roof of your oven.

• **Keep it hot** – you need a high rolling flame that swirls up and over the roof of your oven; have plenty of smallish logs (about 6–8cm/2½–3¼in in diameter) handy to top up the heat every 2 or 3 pizzas. Be prepared to stop cooking temporarily to get the fire back up to optimum temperature. Don't battle on with an oven that's not hot enough. How often you need to add fuel is very dependent on your oven, how quickly it loses heat, how insulated the walls and base are, which goes back to the point of knowing your oven inside out.

• **Choose your fuel carefully** – the low moisture content of kiln-dried timber and eco-logs made of compressed sawdust means that both give out a lot of heat, and I've come to learn that my oven responds best to a fire that's made with a combination of both.

GET YOUR TOPPINGS ORGANIZED

Once you have lit the fire, you need to think about what you might want to scatter over your pizza. The choice is, of course, an entirely personal one, and you can take the flavours wherever you like, but I tend to favour, just as with my dough, keeping things pretty traditional and nodding gently towards their Italian roots. I am unapologetic in saying you'll find no chicken tikka or Tex-Mex pizzas coming out of my wood-fired oven, but if that's what you fancy, go right ahead. It's your dinner, after all.

Whether you stay within traditional boundaries or burst forth into world fusion experiments, it's vital not to overload the pizzas or you risk ending up with a soggy, damp mess. Think of each bite in terms of an intense burst of flavour. There is a reason why olives, capers and anchovies are such key ingredients on many a pizza – in taste terms, you get a lot of bang for your buck.

In the second half of this chapter you will find lots of ideas for different combinations, but here are a few general points worth noting:

• **Cheese** – mozzarella is obviously the norm and for good reason: it melts so beautifully. It's really worth using decent balls of the stuff rather than buying a bag of ready-grated bland rubber. Drain the balls of their liquid and allow them to dry a little on kitchen paper before tearing them into chunks. Allow about ½–¾ ball of mozzarella per pizza.

• **More cheese** – lots of other stronger-tasting cheeses work on pizza. Blues like Gorgonzola and Dolcelatte melt beautifully, as do fontina and nutty Emmental. A good grating of Parmesan, either before or after cooking, provides a big umami hit that is often very welcome.

• **Vegetables** – most of my favourite pizzas veer towards the vegetarian end of the spectrum. Most vegetables benefit from being cooked before being added to a pizza – if you were to put raw peppers or aubergines on a pizza, the base would be cooked way before they were – and roasting adds extra flavour to fairly bland veg like courgettes. If you are roasting vegetables to go on your pizza, think about using the rising heat of the fire to get it done.

• **Meat** – I quite often don't bother with meat at all, but if I do add it I generally stick to cured meats like fennel salami, pepperoni, 'nduja, or strongly flavoured sausages for the intense flavours they offer. For me chicken is too bland, too bulky for a pizza, adding edible padding rather than flavour.

• **Fish and seafood** – I think tuna is great on a pizza, and again it's worth buying decent stuff if you can – use just 3 or 4 generous chunks of albacore tuna rather than a whole tin of watery flakes. Prawns can add a lovely subtle seafood taste, and the bonus is that they cook quickly from raw as the pizza cooks. Anchovies – if you like them, of course – offer a brilliant big hit of flavour.

• **Season everything** – whether you are roasting Mediterranean vegetables, caramelizing onions or blanching purple sprouting broccoli, think about seasoning all the separate components you intend to put on your pizza.

• **Herbs** – a scattering of raw basil thrown over a cooked pizza will elevate it in an instant, while cooking toppings with woody herbs adds a deep flavour – try caramelizing onions with a little roughly chopped rosemary, or roasting squash cubes with some thyme sprigs.

MAKING UP YOUR PIZZAS

The dough's had a second prove, the fire is raging, your toppings and equipment are good to go. Finally it's time to assemble the pizzas, knowing that within a few minutes you can be eating them and the hard work is almost done.

SHAPING THE DOUGH

Time to turn the balls of dough into pizzas, and there are two important things to note. First, don't be tempted to reach for the rolling pin – your hands are the best tools for the job. Rolling will just knock out all the air the yeast has worked so hard to create. Secondly, forget any images you have of Italian pizza supremos spinning a disc of dough through the air, an act of showmanship that is probably best saved for the movies.

While shaping the dough is not a particularly tricky thing to do, it is quite a tricky thing to explain, and there are loads of great videos online if you want to see it done before you tackle it yourself. Like all the best skills in life, practice makes perfect. My first wood-oven pizza was probably a couple of centimetres thicker than I wanted, but it cooked OK and it tasted pretty great – certainly nobody complained. The next time was better, and the third time better again, and now it's a skill that slots easily into my cookery comfort zone. If you struggle initially, have faith that you will improve, and while you improve, remember that pizza actually tastes pretty darn good in all shapes and sizes.

So, here goes:

❶ Lightly flour a generous space on the worktop and also flour your hands, front and back. Take a ball of dough and rest it on the worktop. Use your floured fingertips to press gently all over to give you a flat round disc covered in dimples. Working from the middle, use your fingers to spread out and thin the dough a little more, keeping it a little thicker round the border. Gently rotate the disc as you go, keeping it flat on the worktop so it stays in as circular a shape as possible.

❷ Once you have a disc of about 20cm (8in), re-flour the tops of your hands and slide them under the dough, raising it just a few centimetres (an inch or so) above the worktop. Keep rotating the dough, sliding your hands from the centre to the outside and allowing a little gravity to let the dough stretch down over your hands. If you see it getting too thin in places, move on to a thicker spot. Stop when it feels a few millimetres (about ¼in) thick, take it as thin as you dare, but try to keep a thicker border all the way round to form the edge crust – so useful for holding on to!

❸ If you find your dough is shrinking back instead of staying stretched, simply stop and leave it for a minute or two. Letting the dough relax a little before carrying on can make the difference between a stubbornly thick, doughy pizza base and a perfectly thin crisp one. You can move on to another ball of dough while it rests.

TOPPING YOUR PIZZAS

1 Take your pizza base and rest it on a lightly floured wooden peel. You need to add the toppings when it's on the peel – do it while it's on the worktop and the whole lot will slide off when you go to transfer it. It's a great idea to have two or even three wooden peels so you can make up and cook the pizzas in quick rotation, or you can make your life easy and use foil (see below).

2 Add a good tablespoon of your base sauce to your pizza base, spreading it out in a swirl but leaving a clear border around the edge. Sprinkle over your chosen toppings, trying your hardest to exercise some restraint. Consider a little extra seasoning by way of salt flakes, freshly ground black pepper or a little dried chilli, and finish with a drizzle of olive oil.

3 Once your pizza is topped and ready to go, you want to get it into the oven as quickly as possible. If it sits on the peel for even a few minutes it may well stick and you will end up with a mess. Aim to get it topped and off the peel into the oven in less than 60 seconds.

To get the pizza off the peel and into an oven that's running at an alarming 350–400°C (660–715°F) takes practice and confidence. Lift the peel and slide it into the oven halfway between the door and the fire, then in one swift motion quickly shove the peel forward and pull it back almost instantly. So the pizza stays put, landing on the base of the oven just in front of, but not in, the fire and the peel is removed, almost like pulling out a tablecloth from a laid table! I have affectionately come to term this motion 'shuffing' the pizza off the peel. I hope that word comes to make sense to you...

HOW TO CHEAT WHEN MAKING MULTIPLE PIZZAS FOR A CROWD

In the artisan world of proper pizza-making, pizza is always 'bare baked' – that is, it is cooked directly on the stone of the oven floor.

While I'm all for authentic, I'm even more in favour of just getting the job done. If you have a horde of people lined up waiting for pizza, all you are really concerned with is getting the thing cooked without burning it or flipping it over. In my book it's fine to do the things that make life as easy as possible.

So, the solution is tin foil. Cut a few pizza-size squares and assemble the pizzas on those, lightly flouring them before you add the dough, just as you would if it were a wooden peel. Then use the peel to slide the pizza on its foil into the oven. After about a minute the dough will have 'set' and you will be able to slide the pizza out

using a metal peel, remove the foil and slide it back in to finish cooking. You can then reuse the foil to cook more pizzas.

I find this foil trick invaluable if you have kids who want to make their own pizzas. Many children (I'm pointing my finger at you, darling daughter of mine . . .) can exercise no restraint when faced with bowls of sauce, mozzarella, salami, olives, and the result is often a right old dog's breakfast. But it's a mess they'll enjoy making themselves, and I'm all for firing up enthusiasm for cooking. If the cooking process is started off on foil, they don't get disheartened by the failure of stuck pizza. Everyone's a winner.

COOKING YOUR PIZZAS

My pizza oven is supposedly big enough to cook two pizzas at a time. With an internal diameter of 75cm (30in) in theory that is possible, but in practice I find it a challenge. The intense flame and radiant heat mean you need to be super-vigilant and rotate your pizza through 90 degrees every 30 seconds, otherwise it will burn on one side and remain uncooked on the other. I have found that to do this with any efficiency you need room to manoeuvre, and having a second pizza in the oven just risks burning both of them. Better then to cook one at a time, with a focus on getting each one right, than be disappointed with your results.

To move a pizza around in the oven, slide the metal peel under one quarter of the pizza – if you are right-handed, this will be the front quarter nearest your right hand. With one quick motion, you pull the pizza round to the left so it spins through a quarter turn. Do this every 30 seconds or so, until all four quarters of your pizza are cooked. Adjust the frequency of your turns to match the heat your fire is giving you.

I'll be completely honest, mastering this motion is not easy – there's a distinct knack to it that only really comes with time and practice.

MY FAVOURITE TOPPINGS

I don't want to give hard and fast recipes for specific pizzas here, but hopefully in the following few pages there will be plenty of inspiration

Less is definitely more when it comes to topping a pizza. Don't be tempted to overload the base – each bite should have a little of something tasty on it, not a combination of all the things you've added. This is why seasoning all the toppings individually as you roast them is important, to maximize flavour potential, as is drizzling with olive oil just before they go in the oven.

12 TOMATO-BASED PIZZA IDEAS

ANCHOVIES, GARLIC, OREGANO, MOZZARELLA

To a base of tomato sauce, add a handful of anchovy fillets. Scatter over a finely sliced clove of garlic and a sprinkle of oregano – fresh leaves or dried – and dot the top with a few generous lumps of mozzarella, 4 or 5 pieces torn from a ball. Add a sprinkle of dried chilli flakes for extra punch, season with a little pepper and drizzle with oil before cooking.

'NDUJA, ROCKET, RICOTTA

'Nduja is a spreadable and rather fiery salami. It's seriously addictive and it's brill on pizzas, where it sort of melts into an intense savoury chilli hit. It works really well with all sorts of pizza toppings, so try it in other combinations too. Find it online or, increasingly, in larger supermarkets.

Spread the base with a little tomato sauce and dot little cubes of 'nduja on top, about 30–40g (¼ cup) or so. Bake in the oven in the normal way, then, while it's still piping hot, add a few teaspoons of ricotta cheese and a big handful of rocket leaves. Drizzle over a little extra virgin olive oil, add a grind of black pepper, and eat immediately, before the rocket wilts.

ROAST FENNEL, GOAT'S CURD, THYME, CHILLI

Roasting fennel really intensifies its flavour and it goes well with soft creamy goat's curd. Use another creamy cheese like burrata or Gorgonzola, if you prefer.

To a thin base of tomato sauce add a handful of roast fennel wedges. Dot with goat's curd, about 75g (¼ cup). Sprinkle on some fresh thyme leaves and a pinch of dried chilli flakes. Season with a grind of salt and pepper and add a good drizzle of olive oil.

FOR THE ROAST FENNEL: Spread out thinly sliced fennel wedges on a baking sheet, drizzle with olive oil, and season with salt and pepper and a few chilli flakes. Slide into a hot oven and roast for 20–25 minutes, until soft and lightly caramelized.

OVEN-DRIED TOMATOES, SPINACH, EGG, MOZZARELLA, PARMESAN

I love putting an egg on a pizza, and for a long time the Fiorentina was my pizza of choice at a rather well-known pizza restaurant. Now that I've mastered my own pizza-making in the wood-fired oven, this is still one of my very favourite combinations.

Top your pizza base with a little tomato sauce and dot spoonfuls of seasoned spinach around the edge to create a 'wall' to hold the egg in. Add about 4–5 oven-dried tomato halves around the edge (see page 182), or use 'semi-dried' tomatoes from a deli counter, along with a few chunks of mozzarella torn from a ball. Just before sliding it into the oven, crack an egg into the centre and season the top with salt and pepper. Slide the pizza into the oven to cook. Once it's out of the oven, scatter over a few shavings of Parmesan.

FOR THE SPINACH: Wash a couple of handfuls of spinach per pizza, shake dry and tip into a saucepan. Cover with a lid and set over a medium–low heat to wilt for a few minutes. Scoop into a sieve, set aside to cool a little, then press the spinach firmly to squeeze out as much water as possible. Place in a bowl, stir in a drizzle of olive oil, and season with salt and pepper.

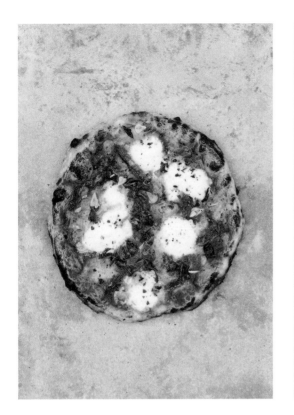

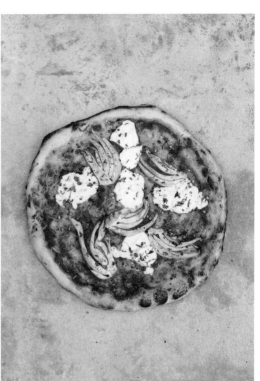

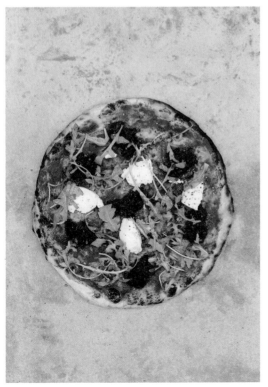

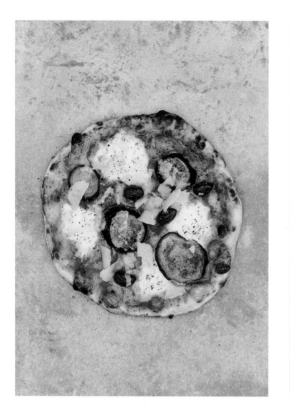
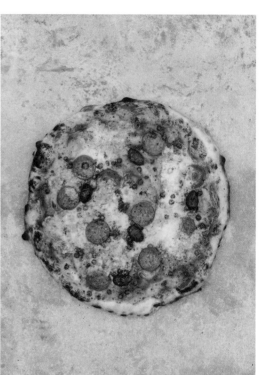
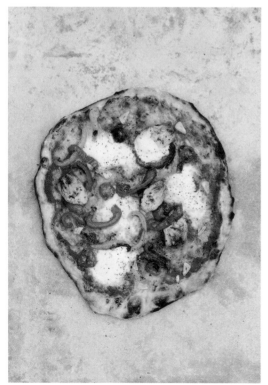
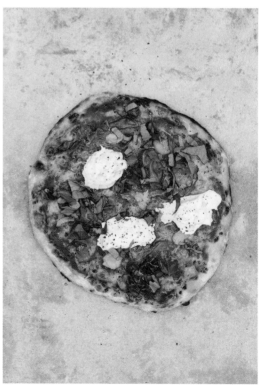

GRILLED AUBERGINE, BLACK OLIVES, MOZZARELLA, PARMESAN

Top a pizza base with a little tomato sauce and a few torn pieces of mozzarella. Add 3 or 4 slices of grilled aubergine (eggplant). Scatter over a few black olives and drizzle over a little oil before cooking. Once the pizza is cooked, sprinkle over plenty of Parmesan shavings.

FOR THE GRILLED AUBERGINE: Slice an aubergine into 5–6mm (¼in) rounds and spread out on a roasting tray. Drizzle generously with olive oil, a good 2 tablespoons, and season well with salt and pepper. Cook for 15–20 minutes, turning over halfway through, until soft and lightly charred in places. One medium aubergine is enough to top 2 pizzas.

PEPPERONI, DOLCELATTE, CAPERS, BLACK OLIVES

Pepperoni is an enduring favourite in our house and in combination with blue cheese, salty capers and olives this is a delicious, intense pizza.

Spread your pizza base with a little tomato sauce, top with 8–10 slices of spicy pepperoni and add 4 or 5 chunks of Dolcelatte, about 75g (⅓ cup) or so. Scatter over a teaspoon or two of capers and a few black olives, season and drizzle over a little oil before sliding it into the oven.

ROAST PEPPERS, CHERRY TOMATOES, ARTICHOKES, GARLIC, MOZZARELLA

Spread your base with a little tomato sauce and add a few roast pepper tangles, roast cherry tomatoes and marinated artichokes from a jar. Scatter over a thinly sliced clove of garlic and a few pieces of torn mozzarella. Season and drizzle with olive oil.

FOR THE ROAST PEPPERS: Deseed a large pepper and slice it into 1cm (½in) thick lengths. Place in a roasting tin, drizzle over a little olive oil and season with salt and pepper. Roast for about 15–20 minutes, stirring once or twice to make sure they are cooking evenly. One large pepper is enough to top a couple of pizzas..

FOR THE ROAST CHERRY TOMATOES: Place a few vines of cherry tomatoes in a roasting tin and drizzle over a little olive oil. Season with salt and pepper and slide into the oven to roast for about 15–20 minutes. Allow about 5 roast tomatoes per pizza, perhaps a little fewer if you are combining them with other vegetable toppings.

SPECK, ROAST GARLIC, BURRATA, BASIL

Burrata is a supremely rich, creamy mozzarella-type cheese that's best used after cooking, as it's quite liquid, so would melt to a soggy mess in the oven.

Spread your pizza base with a little tomato sauce and ribbon over 2 or 3 slices of speck (or use prosciutto if you prefer). Dot over a few little blobs of unctuous roast garlic, season well with plenty of pepper and a good drizzle of olive oil, then slide into the oven to bake. As soon as you pull it from the oven, scatter over a few generous pieces torn from a ball of creamy burrata and throw on a generous handful of roughly chopped basil leaves. Another drizzle of olive oil wouldn't go amiss.

FOR THE ROAST GARLIC: Simply put a whole, preferably large, bulb of garlic into a small roasting tin or on a metal plate and slide into the oven to roast for about 25–30 minutes, turning frequently so it roasts evenly. The skin should be blackened in places, and the bulb will yield softly when you give it a squish. Leave to cool a little in the skin before squeezing out the garlic flesh and using little dots of it on your pizzas.

GARLIC MUSHROOMS, SMOKED PANCETTA, MOZZARELLA

To a thin base layer of tomato sauce, add a handful of garlic mushrooms. Top with a scattering of smoked pancetta cubes, about 40g (⅓ cup) – uncooked is fine, as they crisp up pretty quickly. Add some torn mozzarella and season with a little salt and plenty of pepper. Drizzle over a little olive oil before sliding into the oven.

FOR THE GARLIC MUSHROOMS: Tear about 250g (9oz) of mushrooms (enough to top 2 or 3 pizzas) into small bite-sized pieces and spread out on a baking tray. You can slice them neatly if you prefer, but I like the increased surface area of a jagged tear. Either way, scatter over a couple of finely chopped garlic cloves, drizzle over olive oil and dot with a few cubes of butter, about 25g (2 tablespoons). Season well with salt and pepper. You could also add a few sprigs of thyme if you like. Slide into a hot oven and roast for about 10 minutes, stirring halfway through.

PURPLE SPROUTING, SAUSAGE, FONTINA

Fontina is a strong cheese that melts beautifully, which is why it's one of the main cheeses in a fondue. If you can't find it, use a mature Emmental or Gouda.

Trim 2 or 3 spears of purple sprouting broccoli and blanch them in salted boiling water. Drain well. Chop a couple of chipolata-style sausages (I like Italian fennel and chilli) into 2–3cm (¾–1¼in) lengths and fry for about 10 minutes, until starting to crisp (or roast them in your oven as it comes up to pizza temperature). Spread a little tomato sauce on your pizza base and top with the blanched purple sprouting and the fried sausage pieces. Add a few generous cubes of fontina (about 50–60g/ ½ cup) and season with a little salt and pepper. Drizzle with a little olive oil and slide into the oven.

SPICED MEAT, PICKLED RED ONION, CORIANDER, TAHINI DRESSING

This cheese-free pizza is inspired by lahmacun, a delicious Turkish spiced-meat flatbread. If you can't resist cheese, you could sprinkle over a little feta before cooking.

A couple of hours before you want to cook your pizza, prepare the toppings. Mix 100g (½ cup) of minced beef or lamb with a crushed clove of garlic, a good pinch each of chilli flakes, ground allspice and ground cumin, and a little chopped fresh flat-leaf parsley. Season well with salt and pepper and set aside to marinate in the fridge. Make a tahini dressing by stirring a tablespoon of tahini with a tablespoon each of lemon juice and plain yoghurt, seasoning to taste. Thinly slice a small red onion into half-moons, place in a small dish, pour over a couple of tablespoons of red wine vinegar and set aside.

To assemble, spread your pizza base with tomato sauce and sprinkle over the spiced meat. Drizzle over plenty of olive oil and slide into the oven to bake. Once cooked, drizzle over the tahini and scatter over the drained red onion slices. Sprinkle over a little ground sumac if you like, for a citrussy spice zing, along with a little more chopped fresh flat-leaf parsley.

ROAST SQUASH, PINE NUT, PESTO, PARMESAN SHAVINGS

Add a tablespoon of tomato sauce to your pizza base and spread it around in a thin layer. Scatter over a handful of roast squash cubes and pine nuts. Drizzle with olive oil and season with a good grind of pepper before sliding into the oven. Once cooked, add a few blobs of pesto and shave over ample Parmesan.

FOR THE ROAST SQUASH: Cut a butternut (or other) squash into 2cm (¾in) cubes, allowing about 100g (¾ cup) of raw squash per pizza, and spread out in a roasting tin. Drizzle over a good slug of olive oil and season well with salt and pepper. You could also add a pinch of smoked paprika or dried chilli flakes for extra oomph. Roast for about 30 minutes, until tender and lightly charred in places. Stir halfway through cooking.

FOR THE PESTO: Toast 50g (¼ cup) of pine nuts in a small frying pan set over a medium heat. As soon as they smell nutty, tip into a food processor and whizz until ground. Add a large bunch of basil, including the stalks, and pulse until chopped. Add 1 roughly chopped clove of garlic, 25g (⅓ cup) of finely grated Parmesan and 3 tablespoons of olive oil, along with a squeeze of lemon juice and plenty of salt and pepper, and whizz to a purée. Store, covered with cling film, in the fridge.

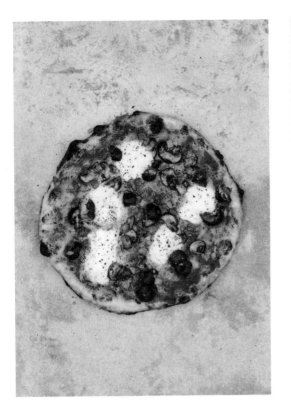

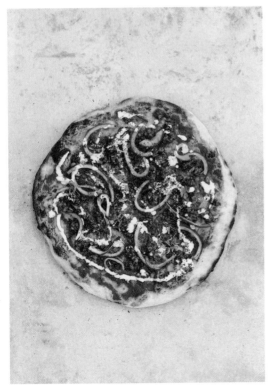
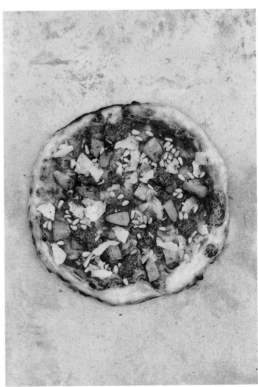

4 WHITE PIZZA IDEAS

If you've never tried a pizza with a white sauce, please give it a go (see page 21), just once – you may be a convert. Creamy and garlicky, white sauce works really well with seafood and smoky, salty things.

CHARRED ASPARAGUS, SMOKED PANCETTA, PARMESAN

Spread the base with a good tablespoon of white pizza sauce (see page 21) and top with charred asparagus. Sprinkle over 50g (¼ cup) of chopped smoked pancetta. Add a few dried chilli flakes if you like and slide into the oven. Once baked, shave over a little Parmesan.

FOR THE CHARRED ASPARAGUS: Snap off the woody ends from a bunch of asparagus and wash well. Spread out on a baking tray and drizzle over a little olive oil. Season with salt and pepper and slide into the hot oven for about 12–15 minutes, until just tender. Makes enough for about 3 pizzas.

PRAWNS, GRILLED COURGETTE, PESTO

Spread your pizza base with white pizza sauce and top with a few slices of grilled courgette (zucchini). Take 5 raw king prawns and score a line down the back of each so they open out a little on cooking – don't worry that they are raw, they will cook fine as the pizza bakes. Drizzle over a little olive oil and season well before sliding into the oven. Once the pizza is baked, dot the top with a few little spoons of pesto before serving.

FOR THE GRILLED COURGETTE: Slice a couple of courgettes into 5–6mm (¼in) rounds, spreading them out in a roasting tin. Drizzle with olive oil and season with salt and pepper. Roast in the hot oven for about 15 minutes or until soft and lightly coloured. One courgette is enough to top 1–2 pizzas, depending on size. You could also add a clove or two or chopped garlic before you roast.

FOR THE PESTO: See the roast squash pizza on page 38.

POTATO, GARLIC, ROSEMARY

It may feel like a carb-on-carb fest, but trust me, potato on a pizza really works, especially in combination with cream and garlic. This is one of my favourites.

Spread a thin layer of white pizza sauce on the base and scatter over the cooked potato slices. Drizzle a little olive oil on top, sprinkle over a few rosemary needles, and season well with salt and freshly ground black pepper before sliding into the hot oven.

FOR THE POTATO: Scrub 3 new potatoes and cut into thin (3–4mm/1/8in) slices. Put into a small saucepan, add a pinch of salt and cover with boiling water. Boil for 5 minutes, until just tender. Drain well, then set aside.

CARAMELIZED ONIONS, TUNA, CAPERS

In an ideal world you would splash out and use a good-quality dense-fleshed albacore tuna for this pizza.

Top the base with a good tablespoon of white pizza sauce, then sprinkle over a couple of teaspoons of caramelized onions. Top with about 75g (½ cup) of good-quality tuna, flaked into chunks, and scatter over a teaspoon or two of capers. Add a good grind of black pepper and a drizzle of olive oil before sliding into the oven. Sprinkle over chopped fresh flat-leaf parsley before serving.

FOR THE CARAMELIZED ONIONS: Slice 2 large onions into thin half-moons and put them into a roasting tin. Drizzle over 2 tablespoons of olive oil and dot with 25g (2 tablespoons) butter. Season well and slide into a hot oven. Cook until deep golden brown, about 25–30 minutes. Keep an eagle eye on them, stirring regularly so they don't burn. Two large onions are enough to top 2–3 pizzas.

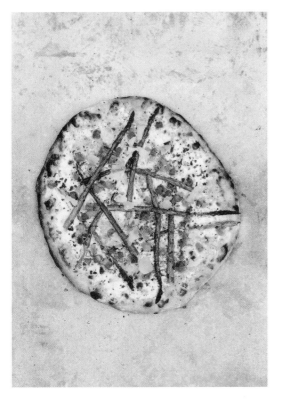

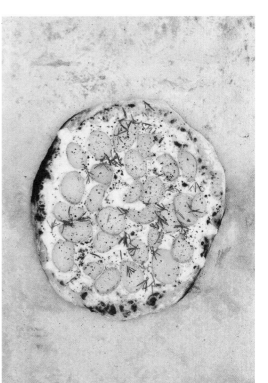

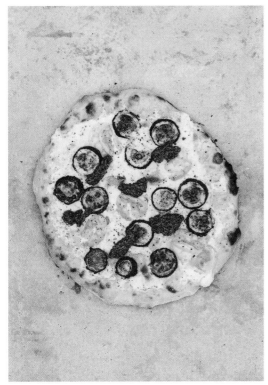

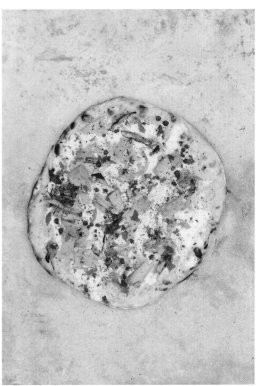

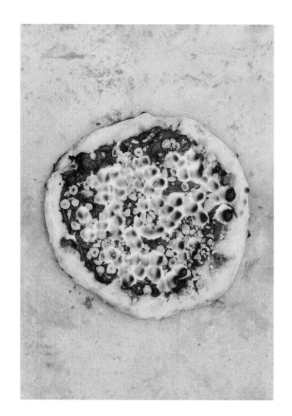
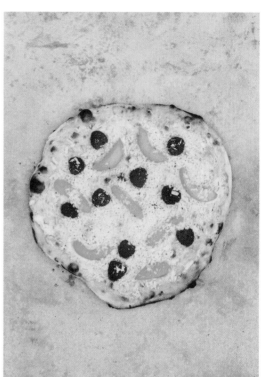
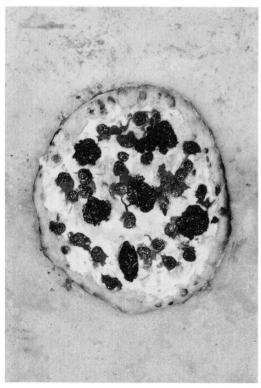
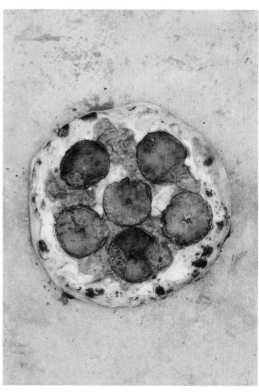

4 SWEET PIZZA IDEAS

Pizza for pudding is supremely unauthentic, but they are pretty fun to make and unsurprisingly they seem especially popular with children . . .

NUTELLA, HAZELNUT, MARSHMALLOW

A classic combination . . . and a sure-fire hit with the kids. Add the marshmallows halfway through cooking, so they don't burn. Keep an eagle eye on them!

Put a generous tablespoon of Nutella into a small bowl and pour on a few drops of boiling water, stirring until you have a spreading consistency. Spread onto your pizza base and scatter over a handful of chopped hazelnuts. Slide into the oven and cook until nearly done, then slide out on a metal peel and scatter over mini marshmallows. Slide it back in for 1 more minute, to allow the marshmallows to begin to toast and melt.

CHRISTMAS CRANBERRY, MINCEMEAT AND ORANGE

A seasonal Christmas pizza, great for using up leftover cranberries and half jars of mincemeat!

Put a good tablespoon of mascarpone or other full-fat cream cheese into a heatproof glass. Pour in just enough boiling water to thin it to an easy spreading consistency, stirring well until it's smooth. Stir in a teaspoon of icing sugar, to sweeten a little, and a little grated orange zest. Spread over a pizza base and scatter over a handful of fresh or frozen cranberries. Finally top with a few little spoons of mincemeat and slide into the oven to bake. Dust with a little icing sugar and a bit more orange zest before serving.

APRICOT, RASPBERRY, WHITE CHOCOLATE

I use tinned apricots in juice, I love them. Do use fresh apricots when in season; you'll need 1 or 2 per pizza.

Put a good tablespoon of mascarpone or other full-fat cream cheese into a small bowl. Pour in enough boiling water to thin it to an easy spreading consistency, stirring well. Spread over a pizza base. Slice 3 tinned apricot halves into 3 pieces each and scatter over the base. Add a good handful of raspberries and slide into the oven. Grate over a few squares of white chocolate as soon as the pizza comes out the oven, so that it starts to melt.

ROAST SPICED APPLES, CARAMEL SAUCE

Put a good tablespoon of mascarpone or other full-fat cream cheese into a heatproof glass. Pour in just enough boiling water to thin it to an easy spreading consistency, stirring well until it's smooth. Spread over a pizza base. Top with a handful of roast spiced apple slices and a few little spoons of dulce de leche or salted caramel sauce from a jar before sliding into the oven.

FOR THE ROAST SPICED APPLES: Slice off the top and bottom of an eating apple, then cut the rest into thin (5mm/¼ in) rings. Spread out on a baking tray and sprinkle over a tablespoon of demerara sugar. Sprinkle over a teaspoon of ground cinnamon and a pinch of ground nutmeg, and slide into the oven to roast. Cook for 5–6 minutes, then use a fish slice to flip the apples over and cook the other side for another 5 minutes or so. They should be soft and lightly caramelized. Allow to cool before topping the pizza, as the melted sugar makes them very hot. One medium apple is enough to top 1 pizza.

2

ROASTING AND GRILLING

250–300°C (480–570°F)

Your wood-fired oven is not only brilliant as an oven, it has the added advantage of live flames and glowing embers that you can harness to roast, sear and grill food to perfection. The fire's intense energy is also absorbed into the base of the oven, which means you can effectively use your oven floor as a hob as well. All in all, once you master high-temperature fires and gain confidence in cooking with wood, you have yourself an incredibly versatile and rewarding bit of kit.

Many recipes in this chapter are super quick – like the mushrooms on page 81, the seafood on pages 51–3 and the cheese toastie on page 67 – and while I wouldn't light a fire just to make them, they are a very delicious way to utilise a bit of the fire's energy. A few take longer – like the Balinese roast pork (on page 83), which needs a high heat to get the crackling going but then cooks slowly, loosely covered in foil, but most sit comfortably within less than an hour's cooking.

With regard to roasting temperatures, I'll reiterate the point I made in the introduction (see page 11) on accurately measuring the heat of your oven; it's tricky, as many variables can skew your measurements. Use the temperatures given as a rule of thumb, and take several measurements using an infrared thermometer across different parts of your oven to gauge an average. This will give you a loose picture of the heat, but I'm afraid it won't tell you much about either the air temperature or the rate at which your oven might be cooling. More important, therefore, to develop your cooking intuition, and if you are adventurous enough to embrace the idea of cooking with a wood-fired oven you are already halfway there.

ROASTING

Roasting in a wood oven is not like using a fan oven – there are no knobs to twiddle to raise or lower the heat, and no fan to circulate that heat evenly. You need to learn to be acutely aware of where the heat is, how the flames affect the food and where your oven's cool spots are. Just like cooking perfect pizzas in the previous chapter, this is a skill you will get better at every time you use your oven.

In terms of roasting equipment, you don't really need anything special – most of my kitchen roasting tins, baking trays, saucepans and cast-iron casseroles are used in both my wood oven and my kitchen oven. Of all my cooking paraphernalia, cast iron is probably at most risk of damage from overheating, as it can crack under very intense heat. I probably wouldn't push my most expensive cast-iron casserole directly into a raging flame, but I would certainly use it happily up to a temperature of 300°C (570°F) or so. Thick steel pans, like the paella pan you can see on page 89, are ideal – very robust and hardwearing and naturally non-stick if they are well seasoned (see page 12 for seasoning advice).

GRILLING

To turn your oven into a grill, you need to use a shovel or metal peel to pull the embers out of the fire into a level bed across the oven floor. Then find something that you can rest over the embers, like a grill, effectively turning your oven into a barbecue. You can buy what is known as a Tuscan grill, which is a sturdy bit of cast-iron kit, basically a grill on legs, that is designed specifically for this purpose.

If you don't want to buy a specific Tuscan grill for your oven, you can easily improvise, which is what I do. I use a deep fish cage inverted upside down over the embers and it works brilliantly (you can see a picture of my grill on page 13). You could also experiment with a heavyweight grill pinched from your barbecue, or use a cast-iron griddle pan (provided any handles are heatproof, so not wooden or plastic). Even something like a long-legged metal grill from a combination microwave or a sturdy cake-cooling rack could work, provided it's just plain metal without a non-stick coating.

Whatever you choose to grill on, the number one golden rule is to set it over the glowing embers and allow it to get really hot for a good 10 minutes or so before putting food on to it. The sizzle as the food hits the grill should be clearly audible, creating an instant seal between grill and food that means your kebabs, or fish, or whatever you are cooking doesn't stick.

SMOKE AND FLAVOUR

People often assume that everything you eat from a wood oven will taste of smoke, but this is absolutely not the case. If your wood is a touch damp, your oven will smoke and that smoke will get absorbed into your food, but in a well-fired oven, smoke isn't an issue. Sometimes, of course, you will want to add smoke (the smoked prawns on page 56 are a case in point), and that's where you can reach for smoking chips. There are loads of products out there designed for smoking food. For your wood oven, as opposed to a specially designed hot or cold smoker, I would use fairly chunky wood chips rather than smoking sawdust, which will burn too quickly at a high heat. Soak the wood chips in a bowl or bucket of cold water for an hour before throwing them on to your fire just before you add the food.

KEEPING THINGS HOT

You can't just turn up the dial if the oven is not hot enough, and as the majority of recipes in this chapter fall within a hot to very hot range – 250-350°C (480-660°C) – it's important to know how to raise the heat if you need to. You can add thin (6-8cm/2½-3in thick) logs as you are going along if there is plenty of flame already, but if your fire has died back too much, you may be better chucking in a few twigs of kindling to get things going again quickly.

A little puff on a copper pipe (see page 12) is invaluable for getting freshly added wood to catch quickly, thereby minimizing possible smokiness. At first, while you get to gauge the strength of puff you need, it's probably best to remove all food before blowing or you risk sprinkling ash on it. But with time and practice, you may be able to get the end of the pipe really close to the fire and blow gently in a very directional way so that there is no ash spray.

The other way to give your food an instant heat boost is to get into the habit of moving the fire around the oven from time to time. The area under the fire will be really hot and can be just what a sulking tray of roast vegetables needs. Conversely, you can cover dishes with a loose tent of foil if they are catching on top or cooking too quickly. This isn't cheating, it's working with the fire to get the food on the table.

GRILLED MACKEREL, HASSELBACK POTATOES AND SAMPHIRE

If ever there was a fish utterly suited to the wood fire it is mackerel, its oily flesh charring to perfection over glowing embers. Stuffed with rosemary and lemon, the aromas alone will transport you back to holiday barbecues. I love these crunchy Hasselback potatoes, probably one of my favourite things to do with a bag of new potatoes, the multitude of thin slits in the skin increasing the surface area and maximizing crispy potential. Samphire, a salty sea vegetable, isn't the easiest of things to source – you can sometimes find it in supermarkets but your best bet is a good fishmonger.

320–340°C (600–645°F)
SERVES 4

800–900g (1lb 12oz–2lb) new
　　potatoes
4 tbsp olive oil
200g (7oz) samphire
4 good-sized mackerel, gutted
　　(about 350g/12oz each)
2 cloves of garlic, chopped
1 lemon, sliced
4 sprigs of fresh rosemary
salt and freshly ground black
　　pepper

Take a potato and lay it on a chopping board. Use a sharp knife to carefully cut slices three-quarters of the way through, all the way along the potato, about 2mm (⅛ in) apart. Make sure you don't cut all the way through – the slices should all remain attached at the base. Repeat with the rest of the potatoes, putting them into a roasting tin as you go. Drizzle over most of the olive oil and season with plenty of black pepper, tossing to mix. Hold off on the salt, as samphire is intensely salty. You can get the potatoes prepped about an hour before you cook, providing they are well coated with oil. When you are ready to cook, slide the potatoes into the oven and leave to roast for 20–25 minutes.

Put the samphire into a bowl and toss with the rest of the olive oil, seasoning with a grind of pepper as you go. Set aside.

Make a few deep diagonal cuts along each side of the fish, then rub the garlic into the slits. Stuff the lemon slices and rosemary sprigs into each gut cavity and season the outside of each fish with a little salt and plenty of black pepper.

Remove the potatoes from the oven and set aside while you cook the fish. Use the metal peel to bring a good bed of embers into the centre of the fire and rest your grill over them. Allow it to heat up for 5 minutes, then slide it out, lay the mackerel on it and lift the grill on to the embers. Grill the fish for 5 minutes on each side, then transfer them to a serving plate and loosely cover with foil to keep warm while you finish the potatoes. If you have a fish cage it is really useful for turning the fish over in one go, but do make sure you heat it up on the grill before adding the fish to it, as this will prevent them sticking.

Use the metal peel to push the embers back into the corner of the oven. Scatter the samphire around the potatoes and slide the tray on to the hot spot where the embers were. The samphire will take just 5 minutes or so to roast – you want it to have plenty of crunch. Rest the grilled mackerel on the vegetables and take to the table.

AND ANOTHER THING...

● If you can't get hold of samphire, feel free to substitute a handful or two of green beans, but they will take a little longer – about 10 minutes – to cook.

TWO QUICK SHELLFISH DISHES

Shellfish cooks brilliantly in the heat from a wood-fired oven, and they are just the sort of speedy thing I might make to fuel an afternoon's baking. Get the fire roaring, allow the flames to steady a little before cooking, then tuck in while you wait for the oven to cool to a steady baking temperature.

For both the following recipes you need the oven to be running at a good hot roasting temperature, about 320–340°C (600–645°F), with plenty of bottom heat from the fire base. Have the fire burning to one side of the oven, and just before you slide the clams or mussels in, move the fire from one side to the other with a metal peel. Then put the pan onto the hot spot. The extra oomph of heat from underneath will help the shellfish cook quickly.

PORTUGUESE CLAMS WITH WINE, GARLIC AND CORIANDER

The simplest and most delicious way with clams I know. Make sure you have plenty of bread to serve alongside, to mop up the glorious juices, and perhaps the rest of the wine too... (Pictured overleaf, left.)

320–340°C (600–645°F)
SERVES 2–4

1kg (2lb 3oz) clams
1 tsp salt
100ml (scant ½ cup) olive oil
5 cloves of garlic, chopped
250ml (1 cup) white wine
freshly ground black pepper
a handful of fresh coriander
   (cilantro), chopped
½ a lemon, to serve

Put the clams in a large bowl and cover with cold water. Stir in the salt and leave to sit for an hour, so that any sand and grit is released from the shells. Drain well.

Put the oil and garlic into a deep frying pan and slide into the oven. Allow the garlic to soften for a minute or two, taking care not to burn it. Remove from the oven, pour in the wine and tip in the clams, seasoning well with plenty of black pepper, tossing to coat. Cover with a lid or snugly tucked piece of foil. Move the fire around with a metal peel and slide the pan back into the oven, on the hot spot where the fire was. Cook for about 10 minutes, rotating the pan once or twice during cooking to ensure the clams are cooking evenly. They are done when they are all open; if a few are still shut, re-cover the pan, move the fire around, and slide it back in.

Sprinkle over the coriander, tip into a serving dish and squeeze over the lemon juice. Eat immediately, discarding any clams that have not opened.

CAMBODIAN CURRIED MUSSELS

Based on Cambodia's legendary fish amok, a creamy curry baked in a banana leaf basket, these mussels are fragrant with lime leaves, lemongrass and coconut. I first ate fish amok at the Friends International restaurant in Phnom Penh, a wonderful charity that provides street children with much-needed second chances by giving them vocational training in the cooking industry. Mussels do rather well with the wood-fired amok-treatment, cooking really quickly and staying tender. (Pictured opposite, right.)

320–340°C (600–645°F)
SERVES 2–4

1 tbsp vegetable oil
1 x 400ml (14fl oz) tin of coconut milk
2 tbsp fish sauce
1kg (2lb 3oz) mussels, washed and de-bearded
steamed rice, to serve (optional)

For the curry paste
6 kaffir lime leaves, fresh or frozen, roughly chopped
2–3 bird's-eye chillies
3 cloves of garlic, roughly chopped
1 echalion (banana) shallot, roughly chopped
2–3cm (¾–1¼in) piece of galangal (or fresh ginger), roughly chopped
1 stem of lemongrass, outer leaves discarded, inner ones chopped
zest and juice of 1 lime
salt and freshly ground black pepper

Put the lime leaves, chillies, garlic, shallot, galangal, lemongrass, lime zest and juice into a deep jug. Season with a little salt and plenty of black pepper and blitz to a purée, using a stick blender. Alternatively, whizz in a food processor. Scoop into a bowl, cover and refrigerate until you are ready to cook – it will keep for a day or two if you want to get ahead.

When you are ready to cook, put the oil into a deep frying pan and slide it into the oven to heat up for a minute. Stir in the curry paste and slide it back into the oven for 10 minutes, until fragrant.

Stir in the coconut milk and fish sauce, put the pan back into the oven and bring to the boil, about 5 minutes. Finally, tip in the mussels, tossing them in the sauce so they are coated. Cover the pan with a lid or a well tucked-in sheet of foil. Move the fire around with a metal peel, then slide the pan back into the oven on to the hot spot where the fire was. Cook for about 10 minutes, rotating the pan once or twice to make sure the mussels are cooking evenly. Take a peek when you think they are done – they should be all open. If not, re-cover and cook for a further couple of minutes.

Give the mussels a final quick stir in the sauce and serve while piping hot. Discard any mussels that haven't opened up.

PEKING DUCK

Peking duck is one of my son's very favourite things to eat and we sometimes indulge him, but as the most expensive thing on the Chinese menu it's a rather rare treat. Now I've cracked the making of crispy duck at home, thanks to the high heat in the wood-fired oven, I have total respect for its costliness – this dish takes a couple of days to nail to perfection, as there are multiple marinating, drying, steaming and chilling steps that can't really be avoided. So, not a recipe for the impatient or time-poor, but one that will yield a really good meal if you love it as much as my boy does.

300°C (570°F)
SERVES 4–6

1 x 1.8–2kg (4–4½lb) whole duck
2 tbsp runny honey
1 tbsp Szechuan peppercorns
1 tbsp sea salt
1 tbsp Chinese five-spice powder
1 tbsp baking powder (soda)
6 spring onions (scallions), roughly
    chopped
100g (3½oz) fresh ginger,
    roughly chopped

To serve
about 18 Chinese pancakes
1 bunch of spring onions (scallions),
    cut into thin slivers
½ a large cucumber, cut into thin
    slivers
hoisin sauce

When you are ready to cook the duck, after the marinating, steaming and drying sequence, you need a really hot roasting oven to get the crispiest duck – about 300°C (570°F) with plenty of live flame is perfect.
Set the duck on a chopping board and use a combination of your fingers and the rounded handle of a wooden spoon to ease the skin away from the meat, starting at the cavity entrance. Go slowly and take as much care as you can to keep the skin intact, but if you poke a hole through it it's not the end of the world. Rest the duck on a rack set over a roasting tin and drizzle over the honey, rubbing it in all over to get a thin even layer.

Put the Szechuan peppercorns and sea salt into a pestle and mortar and grind to a coarse powder. Stir through the Chinese five-spice and baking powder and scatter this mix all over the duck, rubbing it well into the honeyed skin. Rest the duck, uncovered and still on the rack in the roasting tin, in the fridge for 12–24 hours to marinate and dry out the skin.

The next day, rest the duck in the sink, still on the rack but out of the tin, and pour over two kettles of boiling water, one after the other, to wash away the marinade and tighten up the skin. Tip the duck upside down to allow any water to drain from the cavity. Stuff the cavity with half the spring onions and ginger.

Line a large bamboo steamer basket with greaseproof paper and use the tip of a sharp knife to pierce a few holes. Lift the duck into the basket, fitting it snugly inside, tucking the legs in a bit so you can get the lid on.

Set the basket over a wok half full of boiling water and steam over a medium-high heat for 1½ hours, topping up the wok water if it is drying out. Allow the duck to cool in the basket, then transfer back to a clean rack set over a roasting tin. Once cold, chill in the fridge for another 12–24 hours.

At this point the duck is (finally!) ready for the wood-fired oven. Remove it from the fridge and scoop out and discard the spring onion and ginger. Re-stuff the cavity with the rest of the spring onion and ginger and rest on a rack over a roasting tin. Slide into the hot oven and roast for about 15–20 minutes, rotating the tin regularly so it crisps up evenly. Turn the duck over halfway through cooking so the underside crisps up too.

Serve the duck as soon as it comes out of the oven, carved into shreds, with the pancakes and garnishes served alongside for people to help themselves.

SMOKED GRILLED PRAWNS, WITH LEMON BUTTER SAUCE

These prawns have a wonderful flavour, thanks to a handful of wood chips thrown on to the embers of the fire just before you cook. Smoking chips are such a simple way to add smoky intrigue to all sorts of grilled foods – just make sure you soak them in cold water for an hour before adding them to the fire (see page 47 for more on smoking in the wood-fired oven).

And turn to page 162 for a prawn bisque soup made from the leftover heads and shells, a great way to get every last drop of flavour from a fairly pricy ingredient.

280–300°C (535–570°F)
SERVES 4 AS A STARTER, OR 2 AS AN INDULGENT MEAL

600g (1lb 5oz) raw king prawns
1 tbsp olive oil
75g (⅓ cup) butter
zest and juice of 1 lemon
1 clove of garlic, crushed
salt and freshly ground black
  pepper

You also need a handful of damp
wood chips (see above).

You need a good bed of glowing embers over which to set your grill (see grilling equipment, page 46).

First, you need to score through the shell of each prawn along the back. It is a little fiddly but worth it, as it allows the smoke to penetrate into the meat. To do this, take a prawn and rest it on a chopping board with the back facing towards your cutting hand. Press down firmly on to the prawn with the other hand to hold it steady while you make an incision with a small sharp knife down the shell, from the head to the tail. Repeat with the rest of the prawns, putting them into a bowl as you go. Once they are all scored, drizzle in the olive oil and toss to coat. Season with a little salt and pepper.

To make the sauce, simply put the butter, lemon zest and juice and garlic into a small heatproof dish; a metal bowl or similar is ideal. Season with a little salt and pepper.

When you are ready to cook, use a metal peel to pull the embers into a low bed in the centre of the fire. Scatter the damp wood chips over the embers and set your chosen grill over them to heat up for 5 minutes. Once the grill is hot, tip the prepared prawns on to it, spreading them out in a single layer. Rest it back over the embers and grill for 10 minutes, turning the prawns over with tongs halfway through cooking. If your grill is on the small side, you may need to cook the prawns in two batches.

Once the prawns are cooking, slide the sauce into a warm corner of the oven to melt – just by the door is ideal.

Once the prawns are cooked, tip them into a serving dish and spoon over the sauce, tossing well to coat. Tuck in while they are hot, remembering to collect the heads and shells in a separate dish if you fancy making the prawn bisque on page 162.

FOUR KEBABS FROM FOUR CORNERS OF THE GLOBE

For all these kebab recipes you need 8 skewers, preferably metal, to thread the kebabs on to, and a grill to cook them on (see grilling equipment, page 46). The oven needs to be fired up to a hot grilling temperature, about 280-300°C (535-570°F), with a deep bed of glowing embers.

TIKKA-STYLE LAMB AND AUBERGINE KEBABS

The marinade for these gently spiced kebabs couldn't be easier - you just bung it all in a jug and whizz it up. Do try to leave the meat marinating for a good few hours if you can, so that the yoghurt can perform its tenderizing magic. The aloo parathas, spiced potato stuffed flatbreads, on page 101 are the perfect thing to eat alongside. I would cook the parathas before cooking the kebabs, keeping them warm by the fire, wrapped in a clean tea towel. (Pictured opposite, top right.)

280-300°C (535-570°F)
MAKES 8 KEBABS, SERVING 4-6

700g (1lb 9oz) lamb leg steaks,
    cut into 2cm (¾in) cubes
2 medium aubergines (eggplants),
    cut into 1cm (½in) thick slices

For the marinade
4 tbsp natural yoghurt
3cm (1¼in) piece of fresh ginger,
    roughly chopped
3 cloves of garlic, roughly chopped
1-2 green chillies, roughly chopped,
    to taste
25g (½ cup) fresh coriander
    (cilantro), roughly chopped
2 tsp cumin seeds
1 tsp fennel seeds
1 tsp ground turmeric
salt and freshly ground black
    pepper

Put the yoghurt, ginger, garlic, chillies, coriander, cumin seeds, fennel seeds and turmeric into a deep jug. Season with a little salt and pepper and blitz to a smooth purée with a stick blender. Alternatively, whizz in a food processor.

Put the lamb and aubergines into a bowl and pour the marinade over them, turning them to mix thoroughly. Cover with clingfilm and put into the fridge for a few hours, ideally overnight.

When you are ready to cook, thread the lamb and aubergine pieces alternately on to skewers, resting them on a plate ready to take to the fire.

Use a metal peel to drag a bed of glowing embers to the centre of the fire and rest the grill over it to heat up for 5-10 minutes. Once the grill is hot, line up the kebabs on it and cook for about 20-25 minutes, turning them a few times until the meat is cooked and the aubergine is lightly charred at the edges and tender within.

CHICKEN, CHORIZO AND HALLOUMI KEBABS WITH BUTTERED SPINACH COUSCOUS

Chicken, chorizo and halloumi, all my kids' favourite barbecued foods stuffed on to one skewer – this recipe was always going to be a winner in our house. The buttery couscous is given a good hit of healthy green with leafy spinach and is a breeze to cook in the oven. (Pictured on page 59, top left.)

280–300°C (535–570°F)
MAKES 8 KEBABS, SERVING 4–6

a bunch of fresh mint, finely
    chopped
zest and juice of 1 lemon
2 cloves of garlic, crushed
2 tbsp olive oil
400g (14oz) chicken thigh fillets,
    cut into bite-sized pieces
2 x 250g (9oz) packs of halloumi,
    each chopped into 8 cubes
1 x 225g (8oz) spicy chorizo ring,
    sliced into thin (5–7mm/¼-in)
    rings
salt and freshly ground black
    pepper

For the couscous
200g (1¼ cup) couscous
300ml (1¼ cups) hot chicken or
    vegetable stock
3 handfuls of baby spinach leaves,
    roughly chopped
25g (2 tbsp) butter, diced
salt and freshly ground black
    pepper

Mix the marinade in a small bowl by stirring together the mint, lemon zest and juice, garlic and olive oil in a bowl. Season well with black pepper.

Put the chicken into one bowl and the halloumi into another, then divide the marinade between them, tossing together to coat well. Cover with clingfilm and leave to marinate in the fridge for a few hours or overnight.

Thread the halloumi and chicken on to skewers along with the chorizo slices. For structural integrity (very important with kebabs!), start with a slice of chorizo, then follow each piece of meat or cheese with more chorizo – its nice solid texture helps keep everything snugly and firmly together. Also, halloumi tends to have a rather irritating crack running through the centre of each block, which means that when cubed it can fall off skewers easily – the best thing is to work out which way the crack runs and make sure you thread the pieces with any cracks at right angles to the skewer, giving them the most chance of staying intact on the stick. Keep chilled until you are ready to cook.

To cook the kebabs, pull the embers into a flat bed using a metal peel. Brush the grill with a little vegetable oil and set over the embers, then leave to heat up for a good 5–10 minutes. Use gloves to remove the grill, and lay the kebabs on top while it's still hot (which will help prevent sticking). Carefully lift the grill back into the oven and set back over the bed of embers. Cook for about 20 minutes, taking the grill out and turning the kebabs halfway through.

Once the kebabs begin cooking, get the couscous ready for baking. Take a deep terracotta dish, or an ovenproof deep frying pan, and sprinkle the couscous over the base. Pour in the hot stock and season with a little salt and pepper. Top with the chopped spinach and dot with the butter. Top with a lid or a snug-fitting piece of foil and slide into a cooler corner of the oven, away from the fire and embers. The couscous will take around 15 minutes to steam to perfection, but the exact time will depend on the temperature of the oven floor where you have placed it. Check after 10 minutes – it is done when the couscous has absorbed all the stock, the spinach has wilted and the butter has melted on top. If it's not ready, re-cover and slide back in. If it is, fork through lightly, re-cover and leave to keep warm near the oven door while the kebabs finish cooking. If your oven isn't big enough to cook both kebabs and couscous at the same time, begin with the couscous, and keep warm while you cook the kebabs.

Serve the kebabs on top of the couscous.

BERBERE BEEF AND GREEN PEPPER KEBABS

Berbere is a heady spice mix from Ethiopia, fragrant with fenugreek, cardamom, chillies and all sorts of other wonderful spices. The list of spices is quite long, and you can buy ready-blended berbere powders, but it's worth making your own if you can – it will be so much more aromatic if freshly ground. These kebabs would go really well with the spinach couscous from the chicken and halloumi recipe opposite, or you could slide the meat off the skewers and into toasted pittas stuffed with chopped tomatoes and green salad. (Pictured on page 59, bottom left.)

280–300°C (535–570°F)
MAKES 8 KEBABS, SERVING 4–6

3 cloves of garlic, crushed
1 tbsp vegetable oil
1 tbsp tomato purée
700g (1lb 9oz) skirt steak, cut into
  2cm (¾in) cubes
2 green peppers, cut into 2cm
  (¾in) pieces

For the berbere spice mix
1 tbsp coriander seeds
1 tsp fenugreek seeds
6 cardamom pods
1–2 tsp ground chilli flakes, to taste
1 tsp black peppercorns
½ tsp allspice berries
½ tsp cloves
1 tbsp sweet paprika
1 tsp ground ginger
½ tsp ground nutmeg

Tip the coriander seeds into a small dry frying pan and set over a medium heat to toast for just a minute or so. As soon as you smell the aromas wafting up from the pan, transfer the seeds to a spice mill. Add the fenugreek, cardamom, chilli flakes, peppercorns, allspice and cloves and grind to a powder. Add the paprika, ginger and nutmeg and mix until combined.

Put the spice powder into a bowl and stir in the garlic, oil and tomato purée to make a thick paste. Toss the meat with the spice paste until it is thoroughly coated – your hands may be the easiest tools for the job here, as the paste is thick. Cover with clingfilm and chill for a good few hours to marinate, ideally overnight.

When you are ready to cook, thread the meat and peppers on to the skewers and line them up on a plate ready to take to the fire. Use a metal peel to pull a good bed of embers into the centre of the fire and rest your grill on it, leaving it for 5–10 minutes to get really hot. This will help prevent the skewers sticking.

Lay the kebabs on the hot grill and cook for about 20 minutes, turning them over a few times until the meat is dark and crisp and the peppers are soft.

AND ANOTHER THING...

● The berbere spice mix is also great for making Ethiopian-style stews of beef or chicken. Try this blend in the overnight brisket recipe on page 175, replacing the vinegar, herbs and spices in that recipe with the spices from this recipe, but keeping the onion, garlic and beef stock.

KOREAN-STYLE CHICKEN SKEWERS WITH STICKY GINGER AND GARLIC RICE

I love gochugaru chilli, a Korean spice found in Asian shops or online, as it adds a citrusy warmth but not masses of heat, making it a good chilli for introducing kids to a bit of spice. The sticky rice is made with sushi rice, which is pretty easy to find in large supermarkets or Asian shops. If you can't get it, you can substitute Arborio risotto rice or even short-grain pudding rice, but rinse them well under cold water first – these types of rice have a higher starch content, which is perfect for risotto or rice pudding but less so for this dish. (Pictured on page 59, bottom right.)

280–300°C (535–570°F)
MAKES 8 SKEWERS, SERVES 4–6

650–700g (1lb 7oz–1lb 9oz) chicken thigh fillets, diced into 2cm/1¼in cubes
3 tbsp soy sauce
3 tbsp rice wine vinegar
2 cloves of garlic, crushed
a thumb-size piece of ginger, grated
1–2 tsp gochugaru chilli flakes, to taste
a bunch of spring onions (scallions), cut into 2cm (¾in) lengths

For the rice
1 large onion, finely chopped
3 tbsp toasted sesame oil
3 cloves of garlic, crushed
a thumb-size piece of ginger, grated
500g (2½ cups) sushi rice
750ml (3¼ cups) cold water

Begin by marinating the chicken – do this a few hours or even the day before you want to eat. Put the chicken into a bowl and stir through the soy sauce, rice wine vinegar, garlic, ginger and gochugaru chilli. Alternatively, put everything into a food bag and squish about well to mix. Marinate in the fridge until you are ready to cook.

Thread the meat on to kebab skewers, adding a few pieces of spring onion widthways as you go. Set aside while you begin the rice.

Take a large deep frying pan, or an even a heavy-bottomed small roasting tin, add the onion, sesame oil, garlic and ginger and season with salt and pepper. Slide into the hot oven and allow to fry for about 10–15 minutes, stirring a few times, until softened and starting to caramelize. Add the rice and water to the pan, stirring well. Cover with a tight-fitting lid or a piece of foil. Slide back into the oven and leave for 20 minutes.

Once the rice is cooking, pull the embers into a nice flat bed using a metal peel. Brush the grill with a little vegetable oil, then set over the embers and leave to heat up for 5–10 minutes. Use gloves to remove the grill and lay the kebabs on top while it's still hot (this helps prevent sticking). Carefully lift the grill back into the oven and set back over the bed of embers. Cook for about 15–20 minutes, taking the grill out and turning them over halfway though.

Serve the kebabs on top of the rice.

ESQUITES (MEXICAN SWEETCORN SALAD)

It's hard for me to describe just how much this Mexican corn salad floats my boat – sweet, salty, creamy, intensely savoury, all with a smoky chilli hit, it is absolutely my favourite thing to make when fresh heads of sweetcorn are in season. Try to find chipotle chilli flakes if you can – they add a deep smoky flavour. Many large supermarkets will have them, and if you can't find chipotle flakes, use a little chipotle chilli sauce instead. This is a fab side dish to the barbecoa beef on page 175 (pictured with it on page 174), and it's also perfect to eat with nachos or a dish of guacamole. Or go the whole hog and serve them all together for a big Mexican feast.

250–260°C (480–500°F)
SERVES 4–6 AS A SIDE DISH, FEWER IF YOU LIKE IT AS MUCH AS I DO!

4 large heads of fresh sweetcorn (corn), husks removed
3 tbsp olive oil
1–2 tsp chipotle chilli flakes, to taste (or regular chilli flakes)
100g (½ cup) feta cheese, crumbled
3 heaped tbsp sour cream
½ a bunch of spring onions (scallions), finely sliced
1 clove of garlic, crushed
a small bunch of fresh coriander (cilantro), chopped
salt and freshly ground black pepper

The oven needs to be fired up to a good hot roasting temperature – about 250–260°C (480–500°F) – with plenty of live flames, but not a roaring pizza temperature.

Take one of the heads of corn and hold it firmly with one end down on a chopping board. Use a sharp knife to slice downwards, skimming off the kernels of corn. You need to get a feel for how deep to cut – too shallow and you will waste corn, too deep and you may end up with woody bits. Scoop up the kernels – they will no doubt have scattered far and wide – and put them into a large roasting tin. Repeat with the other heads of corn. Pour over the oil, add the chilli flakes and season with salt and pepper, tossing well to mix.

Make the dressing by putting most of the feta into a mixing bowl (one big enough to mix the corn through once cooked), along with the sour cream, spring onions, garlic and most of the coriander. Reserve a little feta and coriander to garnish. Set the dressing aside while you roast the corn.

Slide the roasting tray into the hot oven, pretty near the embers so the corn gets a blast of good strong heat. Leave to roast until nicely charred in places, about 20–25 minutes, sliding the tray out and tossing everything around a couple of times to make sure it's cooking evenly.

Once the corn has cooked, tip it into the bowl of dressing, scraping any little caramelized bits in too – they will add bags of flavour. Toss well to mix, then spoon into a serving dish. Scatter over the rest of the feta and coriander.

Serve while hot, or leave to cool to room temperature. Keeps well in the fridge for up to 3 days, but do allow it to come back to room temperature before serving, for maximum flavour.

POLENTA CROSTINI WITH WILD MUSHROOMS, GARLIC AND TALEGGIO

Parmesan-flavoured polenta baked to a crisp base is perfect for topping with all sorts of tasty items for a starter or snack. Here it's topped with an autumnal wild mushroom and melting cheese combo, but see below for some other ideas for using up leftover roast veg. As a bonus, polenta is naturally gluten-free, so these crostini are a great nibble or snack if wheat is an issue. You do need to begin this recipe a good few hours before you want to eat it, as the polenta needs a good long chill in the fridge to firm up before slicing.

280–300°C (535–570°F)
MAKES 18 CROSTINI, SERVING 6–8 AS A NIBBLE

For the crostini
600ml (2½ cups) vegetable or
  chicken stock
150g (1 cup) polenta
50g (⅔ cup) Parmesan, freshly
  grated
25g (2 tbsp) butter
a little olive oil, for greasing
salt and freshly ground black
  pepper

For the topping
400g (14oz) mushrooms, a mix of
  wild and chestnut mushrooms
25g (2 tbsp) butter
2 tbsp olive oil
2–3 cloves of garlic, crushed
200g Taleggio, cut into 1cm/½in
  cubes
fresh basil, to garnish
salt and freshly ground black
  pepper

AND ANOTHER THING...

A few ideas for using up any leftover
roast veg from pizza-making (see pages
34–40, for wood roasting veg tips).
● Roast squash, ricotta, sage
● Roast pepper and shaved pecorino
● Roast cherry tomatoes with
goat's cheese

Put the stock into a saucepan, set over a high heat and bring to the boil. Once boiling, slowly pour in the polenta, stirring constantly so that no lumps form. Reduce the heat to medium–low and continue to cook, stirring all the time, until it's really thick – about 5 minutes. Take a little care, as it does have a tendency to spit molten bubbles. Turn off the heat and add the Parmesan and butter, stirring until it's melted and smooth. Season generously with salt and pepper.

Lightly grease a large baking tray and scoop the polenta out on to it. Spread it out into a 1cm (½in) thick slab, using a table knife to smooth the top. You can also use your clean hands to smooth and press the top once it's cooled a little. Set aside to go cold, then wrap the tray in clingfilm and refrigerate for a few hours until really solid – overnight is fine too if you want to get ahead.

Cut the slab of chilled polenta – it will be really solid now – into 9 evenly sized rectangles. Slice each rectangle into 2 triangles and spread out over a couple of baking trays, making sure they have plenty of space around them. Drizzle over a little olive oil, and turn the triangles over a few times so they are evenly coated with oil.

Slide one tray into the hot oven and bake for 15 minutes, rotating the tray a few times and turning the crostini over with a palette knife halfway through. Repeat with the second tray and set both aside while you make the topping.

Put the mushrooms into a large heatproof frying pan and add the butter, olive oil and garlic. Season with salt and pepper and slide the pan into the oven. Allow the mushrooms to fry in the buttery juices for a few minutes, pulling out the pan and stirring a couple of times until they have softened.

At this point you can set both mushrooms and polenta aside, ready for warming through just before you eat.

When you are ready to eat, arrange the polenta triangles on one baking tray – they can sit pretty snugly together now. Top each with a few mushrooms and a couple of little cubes of Taleggio and slide back into the oven for 2–3 minutes to warm through and allow the cheese to melt a little. Serve immediately, while the polenta is crisp and the cheese oozing.

SPICY CHEESE TOASTIES, WOOD OVEN-STYLE

An insanely good little chef's perk to knock up while you are getting the oven hot for a cooking session or when you have a gap between cooking other dishes, making cheese toasties in your wood oven couldn't be easier. In this version I've spiced it up, as is often my way, with some punchy aubergine pickle, but you can take this idea any way you like. The trick to perfection is buttering the outside of the bread so that it crisps up beautifully.

280–300°C (535–570°F)
SERVES 1

a couple of slices of your favourite bread, cut to about 1cm/½in thick
soft butter, to spread over the bread
about 75g (¾ cup) mature Cheddar, grated
1 spring onion (scallion), finely chopped
a little chopped fresh coriander (cilantro)
a teaspoon or two of brinjal (aubergine/eggplant) pickle
freshly ground black pepper

Temperature here is not that important but a few embers pulled from the fire will speed up toasting considerably.

Butter the slices of bread and lay them butter side down on a plate. Sprinkle the cheese over one slice of bread and scatter the spring onion and coriander on top. A good grind of pepper wouldn't go amiss either. Spread the brinjal pickle on the other slice, then turn it butter side upwards as you press it onto the cheese topping.

When you are ready to grill your sandwich, use a metal peel to pull a few embers into the centre of the oven. Rest a grill over the embers to heat up for 5–10 minutes. Place the slices on the hot grill rack and slide it into the oven near the fire, toasting for a few minutes until the bread is crisp and the cheese is melting. Turn it over halfway through and rotate it to make sure it's cooking evenly.

AND ANOTHER THING...

Instead of spiced pickle and coriander:
• Try a few slices of ripe tomato tucked in between the grated cheese.
• Use a dollop of pesto instead of the pickle, or use traditional autumn apple and tomato chutney instead of the Indian flavours.
• Or try a smear of mustard: English, Dijon or wholegrain.
• Brie, Gruyère, smoked Cheddar, some sort of blue cheese are all good cheese swaps.

THREE IRRESISTIBLE BAR SNACKS

Salty, spicy, very moreish – the perfect bar snack is surely designed to help the beer (or wine, or whatever) go down better, and this trio of tasty items surely fulfils that brief. They are also a breeze to make, and the perfect thing to knock up while you are waiting for your oven to fire up to full-pizza temperature, or whenever you have a slot in your fire-cooking schedule. If you add the savoury shortbreads into the mix (see page 107; pictured opposite, right), you have a mini-snack feast to keep your guests happy as you cook.

DEVILLED PORK SCRATCHINGS

290–300°C (550–570°F)
SERVES 4–6 AS PART OF SNACK SELECTION

300–400g (10½–14oz) pork skin, preferably dried
    uncovered overnight in the fridge (if you make the
    rillettes on page 183, you can use the leftover pork
    skin here)
1 tbsp English mustard powder
2 tsp sea salt flakes

Use sharp sturdy scissors to snip the pork skin into 1cm
(½in) wide strips. Spread out on a baking sheet and
sprinkle over the mustard powder and sea salt flakes,
rubbing in well with your hands and tossing about a
bit to coat.
    Lay the seasoned strips out over a grill rack and rest
the rack over a baking tray or roasting tin to catch the
fat. Slide into the hot oven, running at around 290–300°C
(550–570°F), with plenty of lively dancing flames, and
leave to roast for about 45 minutes. Use tongs to turn
and rotate the scratchings frequently so they crisp
evenly. Allow them to cool a little before piling on
to a small serving plate.
    Best eaten soon after cooking.

SPICED CHILLI CHICKPEAS

260–280°C (500–535°F)
SERVES 4–6 AS PART OF SNACK SELECTION

1 x 400g (14oz) tin of chickpeas (garbanzo beans),
    drained and rinsed, or 400g (3 cups) home-cooked
    chickpeas (see page 179)
1 tbsp olive oil
2 tsp cumin seeds
2 tsp nigella seeds
1–2 tsp chilli flakes, to taste
sea salt flakes

Tip the drained and rinsed chickpeas (garbanzo beans)
into a small roasting tin. You want them to fit in a single
layer. Drizzle in the oil and sprinkle over the cumin seeds,
nigella seeds and chilli flakes. Add a generous pinch of
sea salt flakes and toss about to mix.
    Slide the tin into the hot oven and allow the
chickpeas to roast for about 30 minutes, shaking the tin
to mix them up every now and then to make sure they
are cooking evenly. You want them to be crisp and a
deep golden brown. Allow them to cool a little, then
tip into a serving bowl.
    Best eaten on the day of cooking.

SMOKY ALMONDS

250–260°C (480–500°F)
SERVES 4–6 AS PART OF SNACK SELECTION

200g (1½ cups) whole almonds
1 tbsp olive oil
1–2 tsp smoked paprika, to taste
sea salt flakes

Tip the almonds into a small roasting tin so they fit in a single layer. Drizzle over the oil, and sprinkle with paprika and sea salt, tossing about so they are evenly coated. Slide the tin into the oven to bake until the almonds are golden and aromatic, stirring once or twice. They won't take long, about 10–15 minutes. Allow to cool a little before tipping into a serving bowl. These nuts will keep well in an airtight box for a week or so.

WOOD ROAST RATATOUILLE

This is a really loose recipe, ripe for adapting to whatever quantities of Mediterranean veg you happen to have to hand, and is perfect for tweaking in lots of ways (see below for a few ideas). It's great to make in midsummer when all these veg are plentiful and cheap. This recipe makes a generous amount, more than you need in one sitting, but it keeps well for several days in the fridge and tastes really good at room temperature too, making it ideal for picnics or workday lunches.

250–280°C (480–535°F)
SERVES 4–6

2 aubergines (eggplants), cut into
  small dice
2 red, yellow or orange (bell)
  peppers, cut into small dice
5 tbsp olive oil
3 courgettes (zucchini), cut into
  small dice
5 fat cloves of garlic, finely chopped
750g (1lb 10oz) cherry tomatoes,
  quartered
4 tbsp red wine vinegar
2 tbsp caster (superfine) sugar, or
  a little less if your tomatoes are
  really ripe
salt and freshly ground black
  pepper

To serve
2–3 tbsp extra virgin olive oil, for
  drizzling
a large bunch of fresh basil,
  chopped
75g (1 cup) Parmesan, freshly
  grated, or to taste

You need a good hot roasting oven for this recipe – a temperature of 250–280°C (480–535°F) with some live flames is ideal to get plenty of good colour into the veg. Like many recipes in this book, you can definitely cook it at a lower temperature – it will just take a bit longer and you will get slightly less intense flavours.

Put the diced aubergines and peppers into a large roasting tin, drizzle over the olive oil and season with a little salt and pepper. Slide into the hot oven, near the fire, to roast for 10–15 minutes, taking out the tray and stirring once or twice, depending on the heat of the fire. You are looking to get some good colour into the vegetables.

Remove the tin and add the courgettes and garlic. Stir to mix, and roast for another 10 minutes. Remove the tin from the oven again and add the tomatoes, vinegar and sugar, once again stirring together. Slide the tin back into the oven and cook for another 20–25 minutes, by which time the vegetables should be caramelized, soft and tender.

Allow to cool for 10 minutes, then drizzle over the extra virgin olive oil, scatter on the basil, toss everything together well and spoon into a serving dish. Sprinkle generously with the Parmesan and serve, either warm or at room temperature.

AND ANOTHER THING...

• Add a drained and rinsed tin of chickpeas (garbanzo beans) or cannellini beans along with the tomatoes (or better still, some home-cooked ones, see page 179).
• Toss through a couple of tablespoons of chopped capers or black olives just before serving.
• Add some spices as you roast the veg (a generous teaspoon each of ground cumin and coriander, a little pinch of cinnamon) and you'll have a version of the Turkish dish turlu turlu.

ONE-PAN ROAST SPICED SMOKED HADDOCK, POTATOES AND CRISPY KALE

With its delicate Indian spicing, the flavour inspiration for this easy recipe is vaguely kedgeree-based, but with crispy roasted potatoes rather than rice. It may seem a bit counter-intuitive to use Parmesan in a fish dish, but it doesn't add a particularly cheesy flavour, more of a crisp umami kick. If you don't fancy the curry spices, there are a few ideas for other flavours and other fish below – this is a really adaptable idea for you to run with as you please. If you're very hungry, add a poached egg.

250–260°C (480–500°F)
SERVES 4

600g (1lb 5oz) smoked haddock fillet, skinless, preferably a good 2cm (1in) thick, cut into 4
4 tbsp vegetable oil
2 tsp cumin seeds
2 tsp coriander seeds
2 cloves
2 green cardamom pods
800g (1lb 12oz) potatoes, scrubbed and cut into 2cm (¾in) dice
2 tbsp mustard seeds
3 cloves of garlic, bruised and peeled but left whole
100g (3½oz) kale, ideally freshly torn from the stem into roughly 3cm (1¼in) pieces
25g (⅓ cup) Parmesan, finely grated
salt and freshly ground black pepper

To serve
chopped fresh coriander (cilantro)
mango chutney

You need a good hot roasting oven, about 250–260°C (480–500°F), with some live flame, for this recipe.

Spread the fish out on a plate and drizzle over a little oil, rubbing it in evenly to coat. Put the cumin seeds, coriander seeds, cloves and cardamom into a spice mill or a pestle and mortar and grind finely. Tip over the fish and rub in well. Set aside.

Put the potatoes into a large roasting tin, add a good slug of oil and scatter over the mustard seeds, tossing together to mix. Tuck in the garlic and season well with salt and freshly ground black pepper. Slide the tray into the hot oven and roast for 25–30 minutes, turning and stirring a few times to make sure the potatoes are crisping evenly.

Meanwhile, rinse the kale well under running water and shake dry. Tip into a bowl and toss with the Parmesan and a splash of vegetable oil. Set aside.

Once the potatoes are nearly cooked, arrange the seasoned fish on top and slide back into the oven for a further 5 minutes. Then scatter the seasoned kale around and roast for another 5–8 minutes, until the kale is crisp and the fish is cooked through (it should flake apart when teased with a fork).

Serve immediately, sprinkled with a little coriander and with a dollop of mango chutney on the side.

AND ANOTHER THING...

- Use thick salmon or cod fillets – if they are thin they can overcook.
- Lose the spices and add a small handful each of chopped black olives, sun-dried tomatoes and capers at the same time as the fish. Replace the vegetable oil with olive oil. Scatter over plenty of basil to serve.

TOAD-IN-THE-HOLE WITH AUTUMN VEGETABLES

Toad-in-the-hole – sausages nestled in a dish of crisp Yorkshire pudding – is a classic comfort dish I loved as a child, just as my kids love it now. The key to a perfect toad is getting the pan really hot and sizzling before you add the batter, making it a perfect candidate for cooking in a wood-fired oven.

250°C (480°F)
SERVES 4, PERHAPS WITH SOME LEFTOVER ROAST VEG

For the gravy
2 large onions, sliced
25g (2 tbsp) butter
1 tbsp olive oil
2 heaped tbsp plain (all-purpose)
  flour
450ml (2 cups) beef stock
a splash of red wine (optional)
1 tsp Marmite (optional)

For the roast autumn veg
a bunch of uncooked beetroots
  (beets), peeled and chopped into
  2cm (¾in) cubes
2 parsnips, peeled and chopped
  into 3cm (1¼in) cubes
1 medium butternut squash,
  unpeeled, chopped into 3cm
  (1¼in) cubes
3 tbsp olive oil
a loose handful of mixed fresh
  woody herbs – thyme, rosemary
  and sage
salt and freshly ground black
  pepper

For the toad
120g (1 cup) plain (all-purpose) flour
2 eggs
200ml (¾ cup) milk
8–12 chipolata sausages
3 tbsp olive oil
mustard, to serve (optional)

You need a good hot oven – about 250°C (480°F) – for this recipe. Keep the oven base hot by moving the fire around the oven. If your oven isn't big enough to get two tins in, cook the onions first, followed by the veg, then keep both warm while you cook the toad-in-the-hole.

Put the sliced onions into a small flameproof roasting tin, along with the butter and olive oil. Put the beetroot, parsnip and squash cubes into a separate large roasting tin. Drizzle over the olive oil, tuck in the herbs and season with salt and pepper. Slide both tins into the oven and leave to cook for 25–30 minutes, stirring a few times to make sure they cook evenly.

Back in the kitchen, whisk together the flour, eggs and milk in a mixing bowl until combined. Season with salt and pepper and set aside.

Spread out the sausages in a high-sided roasting tin 23–25cm (9–10in) square, drizzle over the oil and toss about so they are covered. Bring both the batter and the sausages outside so they are handy by the oven.

Remove the onions from the oven, slide the tin of sausages into their place, and cook for 10 minutes. Keep the veg roasting, rotating the tin and stirring if necessary to keep them cooking evenly.

Finish the gravy while the sausages are cooking. Rest the tin of onions over the hob over a medium heat. Stir in the flour until thoroughly combined with the buttery juices, then slowly pour in the stock, stirring all the time as it thickens. Add the wine and Marmite (if using) and simmer steadily for a few minutes. Keep warm over a very low heat.

Once the sausages have had 10 minutes, remove them from the oven and use tongs to move them into a bowl temporarily – they won't be particularly crispy yet, but never fear. Check the oven floor temperature; it may have cooled down too much. In that case, remove the vegetables from the oven too and use the metal peel to shift the embers from one side of the oven to the other. Check the floor temperature where the embers were: you want a good feisty temperature – about 250°C (480°F) is ideal. Slide the vegetables back in, along with the empty sausage tin, favouring the hotter part of the oven for this as you need to get the oil really hot.

After a couple of minutes, slide out the empty tin and quickly pour in the batter while the pan is still really hot – it should sizzle when it hits the oil. Quickly arrange the sausages on top and slide back into the oven as fast as possible. Shut the door, leaving it ajar if there are still live flames in the oven. Roast for 25–30 minutes – the batter should be puffed up and deeply golden and the vegetables should be tender inside and crisp on the outside.

Serve immediately, with the gravy to pour over both toad and roast veg, and a good dollop of mustard, if you like.

FLAT ROAST CHICKEN WITH BUTTER RUB

By flattening out your chicken you are essentially turning a round-shaped thing into a thinner, more even layer, which not only speeds up the cooking time, it also gives you more delicious crispy bits than when roasting it whole. This technique is called spatchcocking, and it's pretty easy to do but is definitely at the hands-on end of cooking, as is the application of plenty of flavoured butter between the skin and the meat. It's definitely all worth it, so embrace your inner cavewoman and get stuck in.

250°C (480°F)
SERVES ABOUT 4-6

1 x 1.8-2kg (4-4½lb) whole chicken

For the butter
75g (⅓ cup) butter, softened
2 cloves of garlic, crushed
salt and freshly ground black
   pepper

Then pick one of the following:

• Tarragon and parsley
2 tbsp fresh tarragon leaves
2 tbsp fresh parsley leaves

• Harissa
1-2 tbsp harissa (either a dried spice
   blend, or ready-made paste)

• Fennel and lemon
1 tbsp fennel seeds, crushed
finely grated zest of 1 lemon

You need a good steady roasting temperature for this roast chicken - about 250°C (480°F) is perfect. A little cooler will just take longer, a little hotter may mean covering with foil to stop burning.

First spatchcock your chicken, which isn't hard but does take a bit of elbow grease. Lay the chicken on a board, breast side down, and use sharp kitchen scissors to cut down one side of the backbone (use your hands to pull/tear a little if you get to a particularly stiff bit). Then cut down the other side to remove and discard the backbone (saving it for stock if you like, see page 182). Turn the chicken breast side up and press very firmly with the palm of one hand to squish it out flat. Now you need to ease your hands under the skin of each breast and each leg. This is easy now you've opened the chicken out, as there are several access points along the cut. Rearrange the legs and wings so they are even and tucked in, and place the chicken in a roasting tin. Give your hands and the worktop a really good wash!

To make the butter rub, simply stir the softened butter with the garlic and a little salt and pepper, then add whichever of the other three flavourings you want to use. Take generous teaspoons of the butter mix and push it inside the chicken, into the gaps you created between the skin and the meat. Think roughly a heaped teaspoon per leg and per breast. Once you've divided the mix between the parts of the chicken, it's time to get your hands in again. Push the butter in as far as you can and massage it about a bit, repeating for both legs and both breasts. Then, with your buttery hands, rub as much as you can on to the outside of the chicken. Wash your hands again.

Season the skin all over with a little extra salt and pepper and turn the chicken breast side down in the tin. Set aside in the fridge until you are ready to roast. This hands-on process can be done up to 24 hours ahead if you want to get the hard work done and dusted.

Once the oven is at temperature, slide in the roasting tin and leave the chicken to cook for a good 45 minutes. Rotate the tin a couple of times to make sure the chicken cooks evenly, but keep it breast down at this stage. Take it out of the oven, turn the chicken breast side up, then slide it back in to roast for another 45-55 minutes, until the chicken is really crisp and cooked through. Check for doneness by inserting a meat thermometer into a nice thick part of the meat - it should reach 75°C (165°F) or above. Check in a few places to make sure it's up to temperature at various points.

Allow the chicken to rest for 10 minutes, then cut it into pieces and serve with the buttery juices poured over and your choice of side dish.

MIGAS WITH TOMATOES, CHORIZO AND BAKED EGGS

Migas, meaning 'crumbs', is a very traditional Spanish breakfast dish of crisply fried stale bread that has become rather trendy of late. Just like paella, it's one of those highly regional dishes that can be contentious and cause cries along the lines of 'My granny only made it like this, so that's the only way.' The heritage of food is, of course, fascinating and important, but the way I like to cook is to use up what I have to hand, grabbing bits and bobs from all sorts of cultures – the British way, surely, to be culinary magpies? So here is my version of migas, unauthentic for sure, but very tasty, very easy and very adaptable.

240–250°C (460–480°F)
SERVES 2, GENEROUSLY, FOR A RUSTIC STARTER OR LUNCH

200g (7oz) stale bread, cut into 2cm (¾oz) cubes (the bread on page 97 is great for this)
2–3 cloves of garlic, peeled and roughly chopped
3 sprigs of fresh rosemary, needles picked
2 tbsp olive oil
about ½ a 225g (8oz) spicy chorizo ring, cut into 1cm (½in) rounds
6 medium vine tomatoes, roughly chopped
½ tsp smoked paprika
2–4 large eggs, depending on hunger
a good handful of fresh flat-leaf parsley, roughly chopped
salt and freshly ground black pepper

You need a good hot roasting oven for this dish, about 240–250°C (460–480°F), with a little live flame.

Put the cubed bread into a mixing bowl and sprinkle over 3 tablespoons of cold water, tossing to mix. Add the garlic, rosemary and a good seasoning of salt and pepper. Set aside for 30–60 minutes, until the bread has softened slightly.

When your oven is hot and the bread has finished softening in the water, put a good slug of olive oil into a heatproof (no plastic handles) frying pan. Add the chorizo and slide the pan into the oven, cooking for about 6–8 minutes, until lightly crisp at the edges. Add the bread, along with the garlic and rosemary, tossing well in the spicy oil, and cook for another 10 minutes or so, until the bread is crisping nicely on the outside. Stir once or twice and rotate the pan to make sure it's cooking evenly.

Add the tomatoes and smoked paprika and cook for 5 more minutes. Finally, make wells in the mixture and crack an egg into each one. Season the eggs with a little salt and pepper on top, and slide the pan back into the oven. Cook until the eggs are set to your liking – about 5 minutes for a set white and a fairly runny yolk.

Sprinkle over the parsley and serve immediately.

OTHER WAYS TO PIMP YOUR MIGAS...

● Make it vegetarian by losing the chorizo and frying a tin of drained and rinsed butter beans in their place, adding a tiny bit more smoked paprika to up the smokiness. Add a little more olive oil to replace the oils released from frying the chorizo.
● Lose the chorizo and fry a sliced onion in its place until soft and lightly caramelized, again adding a bit more oil to compensate. Add ribbons of smoked salmon right at the end, giving them just a couple of minutes to warm through while the eggs finish cooking.
● Add a handful of spinach leaves instead of, or as well as, the tomatoes.
● Replace the chorizo with diced smoked bacon or leftover roast gammon or ham.

ROAST PORTOBELLO MUSHROOMS WITH STILTON AND WALNUTS

Big, juicy flat mushrooms roast very quickly to an absolute treat in a wood-fired oven. You can stuff the middle with all sorts of things for an easy vegetarian dish, and here I've gone for a classic combo of blue cheese and walnuts. See below for a few other ideas – but you can basically shove in anything you fancy, so this is a great recipe for using up bits and bobs you happen to have in your fridge.

230–250°C (450–480°F)
SERVES 2 AS A MAIN COURSE, 4 AS A SIDE

250g (9oz) (about 4 large)
 Portobello mushrooms
75g (¾ cup) walnuts, finely chopped
a small handful of fresh flat-leaf
 parsley leaves, chopped
1 clove of garlic, crushed
1 tsp Dijon mustard
100g (½ cup) Stilton, crumbled
1 tbsp olive oil
salt and freshly ground black
 pepper

This is a really flexible-heat dish – the more heat you give it, the quicker it will cook. About 230–250°C (450–480°F) is ideal.

Snap out the stalks from the mushrooms and finely chop them. Put the chopped stalks into a small dish, add the walnuts, parsley, garlic and mustard, and season with a little salt and pepper. Stir well to mix.

Put the mushrooms, stalk side up, into a small roasting tin so they fit pretty snugly. Spoon the stuffing into the mushrooms, pressing it firmly in. Sprinkle over the Stilton and drizzle over a little olive oil. Set aside until you are ready to bake – they will sit happily in the fridge for a few hours.

When you are ready to cook, the tin just needs sliding into a hot roasting oven. The temperature is not crucial – at 230–250°C (450–480°F) they will roast in less than 15 minutes. If the temperature is a little lower than that, they will take a bit longer. If the temperature is a bit low for even browning, push them nearer to the embers and rotate the dish once or twice to ensure even cooking.

AND ANOTHER THING...

• If you have a few leftover roast cherry tomatoes or strips of roast pepper (see page 37), roughly chop and add them to the stuffing mix.
• Swap the parsley for chopped tarragon, or try a pinch of chilli flakes.
• Hold the olive oil and drizzle in a little double cream (heavy cream) for a really indulgent treat.
• Swap the Stilton for a different cheese – try Brie, Camembert or Taleggio, which all ooze beautifully, or use up little bits of leftover Parmesan, Cheddar or feta.
• Mix in a couple of spoons of cooked beans or lentils to up the protein.
• Scatter over a few roughly torn pieces of bread drizzled in oil.

BALINESE ROAST PORK WITH COCONUT RICE

Based on the Indonesian island of Bali's signature dish, babi guling, this is a generous Sunday roast with a colourful spicy kick. Babi guling is usually made with a whole suckling pig, but here I've used a large, boned joint of leg as a more domestic-size version. You could also use a shoulder joint. The coconut rice is dead easy – just mix it up, soak it and shove it in alongside the pork. This rice would also go well with the lamb kebabs on page 58.

240–260°C (460–500°F)
SERVES 6

1 x 2kg (4lb 8oz) joint of boned pork
    leg or shoulder, skin scored
sea salt flakes

For the spice paste
2 tbsp coriander seeds
5 echalion (banana) shallots,
    roughly chopped
5 large cloves of garlic, roughly
    chopped
50g fresh turmeric, roughly
    chopped
40g ginger root, roughly chopped
40g galangal (or extra ginger),
    roughly chopped
6 kaffir lime leaves, fresh or frozen,
    central rib removed
2 stalks of lemongrass, outer leaves
    removed, roughly chopped
4–6 bird's-eye chillies, to taste
2 tbsp fish sauce
1 tbsp vegetable oil

For the coconut rice
350g (2 cups) basmati rice
400ml (1½ cups) coconut milk
300ml (1¼ cups) water
½ tsp salt

The oven needs to be running at around 240–260°C (460–500°F), with a little live flame to get the crackling started. It's best to get the oven hot, allow it to cool with glowing embers, then generate a little flame with a few bits of kindling that will burn down quite quickly, then continue to cook the joint without flame, just embers.

Put the coriander seeds into a frying pan and toast over a medium heat for a couple of minutes. As soon as you smell their heady fragrance, tip them into a pestle and mortar and crush to a coarse powder. Put this into a food processor along with the shallots, garlic, turmeric, ginger, galangal, lime leaves, lemongrass, chillies and fish sauce. Blitz to a smooth purée.

Add the oil to the frying pan and set back over a medium heat. Scrape the spice paste into the pan and stir-fry for 10 minutes, until rich and deeply fragrant. Spoon the spice paste into a shallow bowl and set aside to go cold.

Once the spice paste is cold, rub it all over the pork, avoiding the skin. Try to push the marinade into the folds of the joint so it penetrates as deeply as possible. Rest the pork in a small roasting tin so it's a snug fit, and transfer to the fridge. Leave to marinate, uncovered so the skin can dry out, ideally overnight and up to 24 hours.

When you are ready to cook, make sure your oven is fired up to a good steady roasting temperature. Throw in a few sticks of kindling to get the flames going, giving the fire a little blow with a copper pipe if it's being a bit sulky. (See page 11 for fire management tips.)

Sprinkle the skin of the pork generously with sea salt flakes and slide the roasting tin into the oven fairly near the flames. Allow to roast for 30 minutes, turning the tin every 10 minutes, so the crackling crisps evenly. Cover loosely with a double layer of foil so the joint doesn't over-brown, and push into a cooler part of the oven – around 180–200°C (350–400°F) is ideal. Allow to cook for another 2½ hours, until the meat is cooked through. If you are using a meat thermometer it should read 75°C (167°F) when inserted right into the centre. Remove from the oven and allow to rest for 10–15 minutes.

Once the pork is covered with foil, begin the rice. Simply put everything into an ovenproof saucepan, stir well and cover with a tight-fitting lid. Leave to soak for an hour, then slide the pan into the oven alongside the pork, where it will bake gently for about 45 minutes. Remove from the oven, check that the grains are cooked, then place a clean tea towel between the pan and the lid to absorb the steam. Set to one side to rest. The rice will happily sit and stay warm for 30 minutes or so.

CHILLI ROAST PINEAPPLE WITH WHIPPED COCONUT CREAM

Roasting a whole pineapple certainly has a wow factor about it, especially if you leave the top on, which will burn and frazzle with a little drama in the flames. The fruit is caramelized with sugar spiked with chilli and a splash of rum, which cooks to a dark golden syrup as it roasts.

240–250°C (460–480°F)
SERVES 4–6

1 x 250ml (9fl oz) carton of coconut cream, chilled overnight
1 tbsp icing (confectioners') sugar
1 large ripe pineapple
5 tbsp dark brown sugar
2 tsp chilli flakes, or to taste
2 tbsp golden rum (optional)

The oven needs to be running a good steady roasting temperature with some live flame and plenty of glowing embers.

Put the chilled coconut cream into a mixing bowl, along with the icing sugar, and beat with an electric whisk until you have soft billowing peaks. You can also use a balloon whisk and a lot of elbow grease! Scoop into a serving bowl and keep chilled. You can make the coconut cream several hours before you eat if you want to get ahead.

To prepare the pineapple for roasting, use a large sharp knife to chop off the top and bottom, or keep the top on for dramatic effect in the oven if you like. Rest the pineapple flat bottom down to keep it stable, and slice down in thin strips to remove the peel, cutting just a few millimetres of skin off. The pineapple will now be left with a load of unsightly brown eyes that you don't want to eat. If you look closely you can see that the eyes are in spiral lines running diagonally around the pineapple. Turn the pineapple on to its side, take a small sharp knife, and cut a deep V-shaped trench down either side of a row of eyes, removing the row in one piece. Rotate the pineapple a little and move on to the next row. Repeat until all the eyes have been removed.

In a small bowl, stir together the sugar and chilli flakes, then, using a combination of a teaspoon and fingers, press this mix into the spirals all around the pineapple. Once you've used up all the sugar, rest the pineapple upright in a small roasting tin and slide it into the hot oven. If you are using the rum, pour it over the top of the pineapple and let it puddle at the base.

Roast for about 20–25 minutes with the door open, rotating the tin frequently. Every 5 minutes or so, slide the tin towards you and use a silicon brush to baste the pineapple with the syrupy juices.

If you have roasted the pineapple with its top on, slice it off before serving. Cut the pineapple into wedges and serve while warm with the chilled coconut cream alongside.

FOUR IDEAS FOR ROAST STONE FRUIT

Stone fruit – plums, peaches, nectarines, greengages, apricots – all roast beautifully and very quickly in a wood-fired oven. I wouldn't light a fire especially for them, but if I have my wood-fired oven running, this is just the sort of thing I might have ready to chuck in, to make the most of the energy the fire has given me. I love having a dish of roast fruit in the fridge for spooning over Greek yoghurt at breakfast time. The oven temperature for these ideas is far from critical: if it's cooler they will just take longer, but if it's nice and hot, you get a lovely deep caramelization to the edges that intensifies the flavours hugely.

230–250°C (450–480°F)
SERVES 4–6 FOR BREAKFAST

Here are four of my favourite flavours. Each one makes a bowlful, enough for 4–6 breakfasts.

HONEY ROAST APRICOTS

Take 500–600g (1lb 2oz–1lb 5oz) of ripe fresh apricots, cut them in half and remove the stones. If the stones are stubborn, use a pointy teaspoon to help flick them out. Spread the apricots out in a single snug layer in a small roasting tin. Squeeze over the juice of ½ a lemon and drizzle on a couple of tablespoons of runny honey. Slide the tin into a hot oven (about 230–250°C/450–480°F) and roast for around 15–20 minutes. Allow to cool, then refrigerate.

CINNAMON ORANGE PLUMS

Switch out the apricots for plums, and swap the lemon juice for the juice and zest of a small orange. Sprinkle over a couple of tablespoons of granulated sugar and a good pinch of ground cinnamon.

PEACHES (OR NECTARINES) WITH AMARETTO AND LIME

Use peaches or nectarines, cutting them into quarters rather than halves. Add a good splash of amaretto liqueur and the zest and juice of a fat lime. You probably won't need sugar, but add a little sprinkle if you have a particularly sweet tooth.

GREENGAGES WITH STEM GINGER

Prepare the greengages in exactly the same way as the other fruit. Roughly chop 3 or 4 pieces of stem ginger and scatter them over the fruit, and pour over a little of the ginger syrup from the jar.

WOOD BAKED PAELLA WITH MONKFISH AND CHARD

Authentic paella is always cooked outside over a wood fire, making it the perfect candidate for your wood-fired oven. The most prized part of this dish is the caramelized stuck-on bits of rice at the base, and you want to do all you can to encourage this to happen.

230–250°C (450–480°F)
SERVES 6

a pinch of saffron strands
3 tbsp olive oil
2 onions, chopped
2 red peppers, chopped
3 large vine tomatoes, finely
    chopped
3 cloves of garlic, finely chopped
1–2 tsp smoked paprika
200ml (¾ cup) dry sherry (I like to
    use a rich dry Oloroso)
400g (2 cups) paella rice
1 litre (4 cups) fish stock
500g (1lb 2oz) rainbow chard
500g (1lb 2oz) monkfish fillet, cut
    into 3–4cm (1¼–1½in) chunks
salt and freshly ground black
    pepper

To serve
a small bunch of fresh flat-leaf
    parsley
1 lemon, cut into wedges

AND ANOTHER THING...

● Replace the chard with samphire,
spinach or peas if you prefer.
● Use another meaty fish in place of
monkfish – chunks of salmon or even
haddock wouldn't be traditional but
would definitely taste good.
● Swap the sherry for dry white wine.
● Add a little diced spicy chorizo along
with the peppers and onions.

You want the oven to be running at around 230–250°C (450–480°F) for this paella, with some lively dancing flames and plenty of glowing embers. Have the fire running to one side of the oven, and once you add the rice to the pan, use a metal peel to scoop the fire over to the other side. Then slide the pan back into the hot spot where the fire was. This will help your paella develop the authentic, but sometimes elusive, sticky golden crust on the base. If you think the oven isn't hot enough, drag a bed of embers into the centre of the oven and rest your pan directly on them for the final 10–15 minutes of cooking.

Put the saffron into a small heatproof glass and pour over a tablespoon or two of boiling water. Set aside to infuse.

Pour the oil into a large (30–35cm/12–14cm) heavy-based frying pan (if you have a paella pan, all the better) and slide it into the hot oven for a minute to heat up. Add the onions and peppers and slide it back in, leaving them to soften and colour for a good 20 minutes, stirring a couple of times.

Add the tomatoes, garlic, smoked paprika and a good seasoning of salt and pepper, and slide the pan back into the oven to cook for another 10 minutes. Pour in the sherry and saffron water, stir well to mix, and put back for another 10 minutes to allow the sherry to reduce down.

Remove the pan, stir in the rice and pour in the stock, giving it a good stir to mix evenly. Cover the pan loosely with foil. Rearrange your fire as described above, and slide the pan back into the hot spot where the fire was. Leave to cook for 20 minutes.

Meanwhile, bring a large pan of lightly salted water up the boil on the hob. Slice off the chard stalks and chop them into 4–5cm (2in) pieces. Slice the leaves across into 1cm (½in) ribbons. Plunge the chard stalks into the boiling water and blanch for 3 minutes, then add the leaves and cook for another minute. Drain well and run the chard under cold water to stop cooking. Squeeze out any excess water and have it ready to take to the fire.

After the rice has had 20 minutes, take the pan out of the oven and assess the heat. At this point, if you think the rice is not getting enough bottom heat, pull the embers into the centre with the metal peel.

Add the monkfish to the rice, distributing it evenly and pressing it deep into the paella, but don't stir it through or you'll disturb the caramelizing layer on the base. Scatter the blanched chard over the rice. Cover the pan loosely again with foil and return it to the oven, resting it directly on the embers to give it an extra boost of heat. Cook for a further 10–15 minutes, or until the fish is opaque and just cooked through. Scatter the paella generously with parsley and tuck a few lemon wedges around to squeeze over as you eat.

BAKED HERBY PORK MEATBALLS WITH ASPARAGUS

This is the sort of dish I make often, a real favourite with kids and grown-ups alike. Using milk-soaked bread as a base to your meatballs might feel a little odd, but it's the Italian way and guarantees a light and tender meatball rather than a heavy chewy one. While this is not a difficult recipe by any means, there are a few stages of pulling the pan in and out of the oven as you add more layers. A perfect recipe, then, for a light and sunny evening where you are just content to hang out in the garden, a true master of your fire, perhaps with a glass of wine in hand.

230–250°C (450–480°F)
SERVES 4

2 tbsp olive oil
1 onion, finely chopped
2 cloves of garlic, crushed
1 x 500ml (18fl oz) carton of passata
1 x 400g (14oz) can of chopped
    tomatoes
1 tsp caster (superfine) sugar
1 tsp smoked paprika (optional)
1 bunch of asparagus, trimmed and
    each stem cut in half
2 x 125g (4½oz) balls of mozzarella,
    torn into 3cm (1¼in) pieces
25–50g (⅓–⅔ cup) Parmesan,
freshly grated, to taste
crusty bread, to serve

For the meatballs
125g (4½oz) slightly stale bread
75ml (⅓cup) milk
1 onion, roughly chopped
2 cloves of garlic, roughly chopped
a big handful each of fresh flat-leaf
    parsley and basil, roughly
    chopped
500g (1lb 2oz) pork mince
1 egg
salt and freshly ground black
    pepper

To make the meatballs, roughly tear up the bread, no need to remove the crusts, and place in a food processor. Blitz to breadcrumbs and tip into a mixing bowl. Pour over the milk, stirring well, and set aside for 10 minutes so that the bread absorbs the milk.

Add the onion, garlic, parsley and basil to the processor and blitz until ground to a pulp. Spoon over the breadcrumbs and stir well to mix. Add the pork and the egg and season generously with salt and pepper. Mix together really well – clean hands are the best tools for the job here. Roll the meatball mixture into walnut-sized balls, setting them on a large plate as you go. Cover with clingfilm and leave to rest in the fridge until you are ready to cook. The meatballs can be made well ahead of time, up to a day before you cook, if you want to get ahead.

When you are ready to cook, put the oil and onions into a large frying pan (a paella-size pan, 30–35cm/12–14in, is ideal) or a deep roasting tin. Slide into the oven to soften and lightly caramelize, about 10–15 minutes depending on the heat, stirring once or twice to make sure the onions are cooking evenly. Add the garlic and slide back into the oven to cook for another minute or two. Pour in the passata and tomatoes, stir in the sugar and smoked paprika, and season with a little salt and pepper. Stir well to mix and put back into the oven for 10 minutes.

Remove the pan from the oven and lay the meatballs on top of the sauce, turning them over to coat. Slide the pan back into the oven for 10 minutes, then remove once more. Scatter over the asparagus, pushing it down a little into the sauce, and top with the mozzarella and Parmesan. Bake for a further 10–15 minutes.

Serve while bubbling hot, with plenty of bread to soak up the sauce.

AND ANOTHER THING...

● Replace the asparagus with green beans, adding them at the same time as the meatballs.
● For the meatballs, replace the parsley and basil with lemon zest and perhaps thyme, rosemary or sage (use less, as these are much stronger herbs) – or try adding a teaspoon of smoked paprika.

3

BAKING

180–250°C (350–480°F)

Baking bread in a wood-fired oven is not a new way of cooking – the ancient Greeks were using ovens that look remarkably similar to the ones we use today – but it is an art that's ripe for revival. Most commercial bakeries, even the small artisan ones, use electric ovens, and so it's down to us wood-fired oven passionistas to fly the flag for the wood-baked loaf.

Just as with pizza, the benefits of wood-baked bread come from the really intense heat a wood oven can provide. In the case of baking, that heat comes not from directional flame and live embers but from the amount of heat you can store and subsequently conduct from the walls and floor of your oven. The mass of your oven acts as a battery of heat energy, so it stands to reason that a well-insulated oven with generous walls and a thick floor is going to bake better than one with thinner walls. Which is not to say you can't bake in less insulated ovens, but you will probably find it more satisfactory to bake smaller, thinner, flatter things – flatbread, focaccia, dough balls – rather than big round loaves.

But this chapter is not just about baking bread, it's about beautiful baked things in general – anything you can bake in a conventional oven you can bake in a wood oven, and here I refer to anything that doesn't need flame or embers as being baked. So alongside bread you will find recipes for puddings, cakes, biscuits and even a risotto . . .

FIRING THE OVEN FOR BAKING

Managing a fire for baking is slightly different from lighting a fire for roasting or pizza-making; as baking uses conducted heat rather than heat radiated from flame, you need to evenly soak the walls and floor of the oven with energy before you begin. While the principles of starting the fire are the same – whether you choose a top-down or bottom-up method (see page 9) – you need to fire the oven for longer and move the fire around more before you can bake. This means more time and a slightly more hands-on approach to the fire than in the

previous chapters, so it's worth thinking about a good session of 'batch-baking', having several recipes ready to bake in succession, to make the most of the extra effort you have put in.

Once your fire has been burning well for an hour in the centre of the oven, spend another 45–60 minutes moving the fire from one side to the other, and from front to back, to make sure the walls and floor are all saturated with heat energy. During this time you can use the oven's energy for roasting and grilling – any of the recipes in the previous chapter can be cooked during this phase of the fire. And, of course, if this phase of the fire carries on longer because you are busy roasting, that's absolutely fine too – really, the longer the oven has to stabilize and develop an even heat throughout, the better your baking will be.

Once you have no more live flame, perhaps just a few glowing embers, you can either use a shovel to remove them from the oven into a metal bucket, or do what I usually do and use the metal peel to shove them right to the back of the oven, spreading them out in a thin line against the far wall. After a quick puff of the copper blowpipe to clear the ash if you are bare baking, you are ready to begin your baking journey.

With a couple of the recipes in this chapter – the aloo parathas on page 101 and the savoury shortbread on page 107 – you don't necessarily need to follow these bake-firing rules, and you could cook them in the rising heat of a recently fired oven as they are happy to cook quickly.

DOUGH RULES

When it comes to baking, steam is a very good thing. Steam and high heat promote 'oven spring', causing the gas bubbles to rise quickly through the bread, creating an airy, light texture and a solid crunchy crust. Commercial bread ovens add steam by an injection system, and in a domestic oven you can pour boiling water into a hot roasting tray. You can also try this in a wood-fired oven, but I find the steam too quickly gets absorbed by the mass of the oven and disappears in an instant. And can I add that you must never, ever, spray water directly on to your oven floor or you risk cracking it.

I have found it more effective to create more steam within the dough itself, by upping the moisture content of the dough to about 70–75%. With a higher-hydration dough you naturally get more oven spring. Allowing the flour to rehydrate really well is also a great help, which is why the everyday loaf on page 97 starts off with a very wet 'sponge' that gets a long slow rise.

Just as with the pizza dough on page 20, most of the bread doughs I make are inspired by baking legend Dan Lepard, whose recipes have shown me that you can make amazing bread without really doing any kneading whatsoever. You need a little faith that it works – when you start you have a very rough dough that looks way too lumpy to ever turn into lovely bread. Each time it gets a little 10-second knead it gets better and better, and by the time it's risen it looks smooth, soft and shiny. Thanks to Dan, I have to say I rarely knead bread any more.

BAKING EQUIPMENT

A wooden and a metal peel are great for baking, and just as with pizza, use a wooden one to slide the raw dough into the oven and a metal one to pull the cooked loaf out. A copper blowpipe is a great bit of homemade kit for clearing ash, as well as directly blowing air at a sulky fire (see pages 11–12 for equipment and general fire management tips).

As mentioned above, a good dough is generally quite wet, and for that reason I would recommend getting a couple of specific dough tools. A metal dough cutter is invaluable for chopping dough up into pieces – lightly flour it before you use it to minimize sticking. It is also the best tool I know for getting stuck bits of dough off your worktop. A stiff, plastic, kidney-shaped dough scraper is another cheap bit of baking kit that's brilliant for gently easing a well-risen dough on to the worktop for cutting and shaping. It's great for scraping out the bowl too.

For all the other baked recipes in this chapter (the scones, biscuits, crumble, cakes and savoury bakes), the same rules apply for the equipment as in the roasting chapter – you can use pretty much anything you already have in your kitchen provided it has an ovenproof handle. Also, because the heat here is not super-directional by way of live flame and embers, you can also use sturdy ceramics, like terracotta or stoneware baking dishes.

DOOR ON OR DOOR OFF?

With most recipes in the chapter it's better to cook with the door closed. You are cooking with no live flame, just perhaps a few glowing embers, so it's fine to starve the oven of oxygen (see pages 8–9 for more on fire management). Cooking with the door closed means the temperature stays more even throughout the oven, with less chance of hot spots and cool spots.

BARE BAKING VS. TRAY BAKING

In the pizza chapter I touched on bare baking, where you slide the pizza directly on to the floor of the oven, and ideally this is what you would do with a loaf of bread too. But in practice it can often be easier to shape your loaf on a tray and slide that into the oven, particularly if it contains extras such as cheese, like the khorasan soda bread on page 106 or the simit on page 103, which would be too sticky to slide off a peel. There is also a certain amount of confidence, and more than a bit of bravado, needed to bare bake, and it's absolutely fine to use trays while you are growing your skills as a wood oven baker. If you are bare baking, your copper blowpipe is the best tool for gently clearing the ash off the floor before you put the bread on it.

EASY EVERYDAY DOUGH, AND 3 THINGS TO DO WITH IT

This easy dough needs very minimal kneading and is started off with a 'sponge', a very wet dough mixture that has a long slow rise to give the yeast a chance to gently work its magic. It is the easy bread recipe I turn to time and time again, and once the dough has finished proving you can process it into various useful things. Here are the three things I most often do with my bowl of dough, but you can pretty much turn it into any shape of loaf you like.

800g (6 cups) white bread flour, or a 50:50 mix of white and wholemeal bread flours
2 tsp fast-action yeast
550ml (2¼ cups) hand-hot water
2 tsp fine salt
2 tbsp olive oil, plus more for kneading

Put half the flour into a large mixing bowl and sprinkle in the yeast. Stir well to mix, then pour in the warm water, stirring until you have a spongy wet dough. Cover and set aside on the worktop for at least 3 hours, or ideally overnight in the fridge.

Once you are ready to carry on with the bread, add the other half of the flour to the sponge along with the salt and olive oil. Use your hands to mix and bring it together as a lumpy dough with no loose flour. The dough will be really sticky, as will your hands – just scrape the dough off as best you can back into the bowl and all the bits will get incorporated back into the dough as you gently knead it. Cover and set aside for 10 minutes.

Lightly oil the worktop and scrape the dough on to it, cleaning the bowl out as much as you can. Add a little oil to the bowl and rub it all over with your hands. With lightly oiled hands, knead the dough briefly, just for 10 seconds or so, gently pushing and pulling it back and forth using the heel of your palm. It will still be very sticky, and quite lumpy and uneven. Scoop the dough back up and into the oiled bowl. Cover and set aside for 10 minutes. Repeat this gentle kneading followed by a 10-minute rest twice more. Each time you do it you will notice the dough becoming smoother and less sticky. After the final light knead, put the dough back into the bowl, cover, and leave to prove for a generous hour or two until the dough has doubled in size.

You are now ready to shape your dough. I usually split my bowl of dough in half, and make one loaf and either the dough balls or the ever useful and very portable bread 'roll-ups'.

A FLOURY LOAF

This is a lovely, regular loaf of bread with no frills or fanfare, but one that is endlessly useful. It keeps well for a few days in a loosely sealed bag. I use a squareish metal basket for mine, which means it comes out with fairly square even sides, but it will happily hold its shape on a flat tray too. You could also make it more of an oval shape and bake it in a regular loaf tin.

ABOUT 250°C (480°F)

Once the dough has finished proving, scrape it on to a lightly floured worktop. Use a sharp knife or a dough cutter to chop it in half. Reserve one half for the dough balls or roll-ups, overleaf, or make a second loaf.

Take the dough and cup it between your lightly floured hands, rotating it round on the worktop and drawing the sides down and tucking underneath to make a compact smooth ball. Dust all over with flour, then place it tucked side downwards on a floured baking sheet or shallow tin. Set aside to prove for a further hour.

Once the dough has risen for the second time, take a really sharp knife and slash across the top a few times. This not only looks pretty but it allows the bread to rise in a controlled way. If you don't cut it, it will have a tendency to burst somewhere else.

Slide the loaf into the hot oven, about 250°C (480°F), then shut the door and leave to bake for 30–35 minutes, until deep golden brown. Resist the urge to open the door for a peek until at least halfway through baking, at which point rotate the tray or tin to ensure it cooks evenly.

Allow to cool on a baking rack before slicing.

GARLIC BUTTER DOUGH BALLS

Use half the dough to make a batch of irresistible dough balls. Who doesn't love a warm ball of dough, crisp on the outside and squishy in the middle, smothered in garlic butter? In our house a tray of these disappears in mere seconds. The trick, I think, rather than using the garlic butter as a dip to dunk the bread into, is to make it soft enough so you can take a brush and douse the hot dough balls as soon as they come out of the oven. Leave to soak in for a couple of minutes, providing you can fend off hungry mitts, and you will be in garlic bread heaven.

ABOUT 250°C (480°F)
MAKES 16 DOUGH BALLS

½ x the easy everyday dough (see page 97)

For the garlic butter
50g (¼ cup) butter, softened
1–2 cloves of garlic, crushed, to taste
1 tbsp finely chopped fresh flat-leaf parsley
salt and freshly ground black pepper

Take the dough and pat it into an oblong on a lightly floured worktop. Cut in half, then pat each into an oblong again and cut each in half. Repeat twice more so you have 16 pieces of dough in total. Shaping the dough into oblongs before you cut just helps you gauge more easily what half looks like, leaving you with evenly sized pieces. Just as with the large loaf, cup each ball of dough between floured palms and rotate it, pulling the top down and tucking under to give you a compact ball with a smooth top. Repeat with all the dough balls, lining them up, well spaced out on a floured baking sheet, as you go. Leave a couple of centimetres between the balls to allow for expansion. Set aside to prove for a further hour.

While the dough balls are having their second rise, make the garlic butter. Mix the softened butter with the garlic and parsley and season well with salt and pepper. Leave by the door of the oven so that it softens to a brushing consistency, not quite melted but very soft.

Once the dough balls have had their second prove, slide them into the oven and shut the door. Bake for about 20 minutes, rotating the baking sheet halfway through cooking to ensure they bake evenly. Brush with garlic butter as soon as they come out the oven and leave to cool for a few minutes before tucking in.

STUFFED BREAD 'ROLL-UPS'

The idea for these came from a holiday to Portugal, where all the bakeries, alongside the world-famous custard tarts, sold 'chorizo rolls'. I discovered these were really simple bread rolls that had a few scant slices of chorizo rolled up inside during the second prove. On cooking, the oils from the sausage ooze a little into the dough, and you have a really tasty simple snack that's perfect for picnics and packed lunches.

Not limiting my 'roll-ups' to chorizo, they are an excellent way to use up bits and bobs from the fridge. They are particularly useful for using up leftover roast veg or other toppings you may have going spare from a previous pizza-making session.

ABOUT 250°C (480°F)
MAKES 8

Take half the batch of dough (see page 97) and pat into an oblong on a lightly floured worktop. Cut in half, then in half again, and in half once more in exactly the same way as for the dough ball recipe above. Stop when you have 8 evenly sized pieces of dough. Roll into balls, place them on a lightly floured baking sheet and allow to prove for 30 minutes.

Use your palms to press each ball into a 2cm (¾in) thick flat disc. Lay your chosen flavourings in the centre (just remember not to add too much or it will ooze out the end) and roll up the dough to form a cylinder. Rest them well spaced out and seam side down on a floured baking sheet and leave to prove for another 30 minutes.

Once they have had their second prove, slide them into the oven to bake for about 20 minutes, rotating the baking sheet halfway through so they cook evenly.

Leave to cool a little before tucking in, as the filling inside will be very hot! Or cool completely, to eat later.

SOME IDEAS FOR ROLL-UP FLAVOURS...

- The original – a few slices of chorizo – or try some pepperoni or a thin slice of ham.
- Leftover pieces of cheese, grated or cubed.
- A few strips of red pepper topped with a couple of fresh basil leaves, a slice of aubergine with a bit of shaved Parmesan on top, a few discs of grilled courgette or a couple of spears of roasted asparagus.
- 2 or 3 anchovy fillets or a few flakes of tuna, maybe with a squidge of roast garlic alongside.

ALOO PARATHAS

These chapatti-style flatbreads, stuffed with a spiced potato mixture, are a brilliant thing to eat with the tikka-style lamb kebabs on page 58. Or serve them as a starter or snack, with chutney, raita or pickles.

250°C (480°F)
MAKES 4

For the potato filling
300g (10½oz) potatoes, peeled and diced into 2–3cm (¾–1¼in) chunks
25g (2 tbsp) butter or ghee
2 tsp mustard seeds
3 spring onions (scallions), finely chopped
2cm (¾in) piece of fresh ginger, finely chopped or grated
1 clove of garlic, crushed
1 green chilli, finely chopped
a small handful of fresh coriander (cilantro), chopped
salt and freshly ground black pepper

For the parathas
250g (2 cups) chapatti flour (or a 50:50 mix of wholemeal and white bread flours), plus a little extra for kneading and rolling
1 tbsp black onion seeds (nigella or kalonji seeds)
1 tsp caster (superfine) sugar
½ tsp salt
150ml (⅔ cup) warm water
1 tbsp vegetable oil, plus a little extra for cooking

You need a hot baking temperature of about 250°C (480°F) for these flatbreads, and because they don't take long you can cook them with a little live flame and the oven door off.

Begin with the filling, as it needs time to cool before stuffing the parathas. You can make it up to 24 hours before, if you want to get ahead.

Bring a pan of lightly salted water to the boil and add the diced potatoes. Boil for 8–10 minutes, until tender. Meanwhile, put the butter and mustard seeds into a frying pan and set over a medium heat. Allow the butter to melt, swirling it around the seeds as it does so. Tip in the spring onions (scallions), ginger, garlic, chilli and coriander and stir-fry for a couple of minutes. Turn off the heat and set aside. Once the potatoes are tender, drain them really well and tip them into the pan with the spiced onion mixture. Use a potato masher or the back of a wooden spoon to break up and combine everything together until you have a reasonably lump-free mixture. Season to taste with salt and pepper, scoop into a bowl, and set aside to go completely cold.

For the parathas, weigh the flour into a mixing bowl and stir in the onion seeds, sugar and salt. Measure the water into a jug and stir in the oil. Pour into the flour, stirring together until you have a soft dough. Tip on to a lightly floured worktop and knead briefly until smooth. Chop into 4 evenly sized pieces, then roll each one into a ball and lightly coat with flour. Set on a floured plate, lightly cover with clingfilm and set aside to rest for 30 minutes.

After the dough has rested and the filling has cooled, you can roll and fill the parathas. Lightly flour a patch of worktop and roll out one of the balls of dough to an approximately 20cm (8in) circle. Add a heaped tablespoon of filling to the centre, then draw up the sides over the top, pinching them together like a little purse, pressing out any air pockets as you go. Flip the parcel over and very gently roll out again, rotating and turning as you roll, until you have a 20cm (8in) circle again, thicker this time. Resist the temptation to press too hard or you risk the filling bursting out. Repeat with the remaining dough and filling, layering the parathas with pieces of baking paper as you go. Chill in the fridge until you are ready to cook.

When you are ready to cook, slide a heavy flat baking sheet or ovenproof frying pan into the oven and let it heat up for 5 minutes. Drizzle in a little oil, then quickly wipe around the pan with a scrunched-up piece of kitchen paper. Add a paratha, or 2 if there's room, to the baking sheet and slide it back into the oven to cook for 2–3 minutes, until crisp and speckled with deep brown patches. Turn over and cook for another couple of minutes on the other side.

Wrap in a clean tea towel to keep warm while you repeat with the remaining parathas.

SIMIT WITH LEMON AND THYME-BAKED FETA

Simit are delicious bagel-shaped bread rings from Turkey, liberally covered with golden sesame seeds and often served for breakfast with cheese and olive oil. Here I serve them with baked feta cheese as I love the soft, almost mousse-like texture it gets when it's hot, perfect for spreading on the crusty bread. Eaten with a salad of ripe tomatoes and a few black olives, this makes a perfectly simple lunch.

220–230°C (425–450°F)
MAKES 4

For the simit
400g (3 cups) strong white bread flour
1 tsp instant yeast
1 tsp fine salt
300ml (1¼ cups) hand-hot water
2 tbsp olive oil, plus more for shaping the dough
1 tbsp pomegranate molasses
2 tbsp sesame seeds

For the feta
1 x 200g (7oz) block of feta
2 tbsp olive oil
a few sprigs of fresh thyme, leaves picked
zest from ½ a lemon
freshly ground black pepper

You need a fire that has reached a high, steady baking temperature of about 220–230°C (425–450°F), with no live flame, just glowing embers.

Put the flour, yeast and salt into a mixing bowl and stir together until mixed. Pour in the water and oil and stir together until you have a ragged, loose ball of dough. Cover loosely with a clean tea towel and set aside for 10 minutes for the flour to hydrate.

Lightly oil the worktop and tip the dough on to it, scraping out all the loose bits from the bowl. Spread a little oil on the inside of the bowl and set aside. Use your oiled hands to very lightly knead the dough for 10 seconds, then put back into the bowl and leave to rest for 10 more minutes. Repeat this 10-second knead and 10-minute rest twice more. Cover the bowl and leave to prove on the worktop for an hour. You can also slide it into the fridge and prove it slowly for 4–6 hours if you prefer.

Tip out the dough on to a lightly floured worktop and divide it into eight even pieces. Take two pieces and roll them into long snakes, about 1–1½cm (½–⅝in) thick. If the dough snakes are springing back and won't stay in shape, leave them for a few minutes to relax, then try again.

Twist the two pieces together like a rope, then coil into a circle and pinch the two ends together to join so they look like twisted bagels. Set on a large oiled baking sheet and repeat with the remaining dough so you end up with 4 well-spaced simit. Brush the tops lightly with the pomegranate molasses and sprinkle liberally with the sesame seeds. Set aside to prove again for another 30 minutes.

Meanwhile, get the block of feta ready for baking by sliding it into a small baking dish. Drizzle over the olive oil, and sprinkle on the thyme and lemon zest. Season with a good grind of black pepper.

Once the dough has finished its second prove, slide the tray into the hot oven. Cook for 15 minutes, then check them, turning the tray around if necessary, so they cook evenly. At the same time, slide in the dish of feta alongside. Leave both to bake for a further 10–15 minutes.

Serve immediately, while the feta is hot and melting.

BEETROOT FOCACCIA WITH GOAT'S CHEESE AND SAGE

This focaccia is a rather shocking Barbie-pink when it's unbaked, thanks to the nutritious and very vivid-coloured beetroot powder, but it does mellow in hue once cooked. Beetroot powder is easy to find in Asian grocers, health food shops and online. If you can't find any, simply leave it out, perhaps adding a little extra beetroot to the topping. Like all focaccias, this is best eaten warm from the oven.

200–220°C (400–425°F)
SERVES 4–6

300g (2¼ cups) strong white bread
  flour
1 tbsp beetroot powder (optional)
1 tsp instant yeast
1 tsp salt
175ml (¾ cup) hand-hot water
2 tbsp olive oil
approx.150g (5½oz) goat's cheese,
  cut into 2cm (¾in) pieces
3 small cooked beetroots (beets)
  (not vinegary), cut into wedges
a small bunch of fresh sage, leaves
  picked and roughly sliced
salt and freshly ground black
  pepper

You need the fire to be a steady baking temperature of around 220°C (425°F), with no live flame, so you can bake with the door shut.

Put the flour, beetroot powder, yeast and salt into a mixing bowl and stir well until evenly combined. Pour in the water and add the olive oil. Use a metal spoon to bring the dough together in a rough ball, then cover and leave for 10 minutes for the flour to rehydrate.

Lightly oil the worktop and tip the dough on to it, scraping out all the loose bits from the bowl. Spread a little oil on the inside of the bowl and set aside. Use your oiled hands to very lightly knead the dough for 10 seconds, then put back into the bowl and leave to rest for 10 more minutes. Repeat this 10-second knead and 10-minute rest twice more. Cover the bowl and leave to prove on the worktop for an hour or two, until well risen. You can also slide it into the fridge and prove slowly for 4–6 hours if you prefer.

Once the dough has risen, tip it on to a lightly floured worktop and pat out gently to a flat squarish shape about 1cm (½in) thick. Lift it on to a well-floured baking sheet. Make a few indentations in the top with your fingers, and into them scatter the goat's cheese, beetroot wedges and sage, pushing them into the dips in the dough. Set aside and leave to rise for another 30–60 minutes.

Just before baking, drizzle over some olive oil and add a few sea salt flakes and a good grind of pepper. Slide the baking sheet into the hot oven, shut the door and bake for 30–35 minutes, until the dough is crisp and cooked through, the cheese is melting and the beetroot is starting to colour a little at the edges.

Cut into wedges and serve. Great with bowls of soup for a hearty lunch.

AND ANOTHER THING...

Focaccia is one of my favourite breads to bake – think of it like a thick, more doughy pizza base, on to which you can press all sorts of bits and bobs to add flavour. It's the sort of thing that would cost you top-dollar in a posh baker's, but costs pennies to make at home using up a few leftovers:

● Poke very thin slices of garlic into the dough, along with some picked fresh rosemary needles.

● Press a few chopped Kalamata olives and cubes of feta into the dough, plus a pinch of dried oregano.

KHORASAN, CHEDDAR AND CHIVE SODA BREAD

I love making soda bread – it's perfect for when you haven't got time or just can't be bothered with a long prove from a yeast-based loaf. Traditionally it is made with buttermilk, but I usually substitute a mix of milk and plain yoghurt, both of which I generally have kicking about in my fridge. This is an easy bake, after all, not one I need to nip to the supermarket to achieve. You do need some acidity to kick-start the bicarb rising – if you don't have the yoghurt to provide this, you can use all milk but sour it first with a tablespoon or so of lemon juice. As this is such an easy bake it's not one I would light my fire especially to make, but if the oven was already hot and I had a cooking gap I could knock it up in minutes and shove it in, knowing it would get eaten or it could go into the freezer for another day.

A fairly new ingredient to me, khorasan flour is made from an ancient wheat variety and is a fabulous thing to bake with, giving you all the goodness of a wholemeal flour but with none of the potential heaviness.

180–200°C (350–400°F)
MAKES 1 LOAF

250g (2 cups) khorasan flour
250g (2 cups) plain (all-purpose)
   flour
1 tsp bicarbonate of soda
   (baking soda)
½ tsp salt
200g (7oz) mature Cheddar, grated
a generous bunch of fresh chives,
   snipped
100ml (⅓ cup) milk
300g (1½ cups) full-fat plain yoghurt
freshly ground black pepper
   (optional)

You need the oven to be running at about 180–200°C (350–400°F) for this really easy loaf.

In a large mixing bowl, stir together the flours, bicarbonate of soda and salt. Fold in the cheese and chives and a good grind of black pepper if you fancy.

Measure the milk into a jug and add the yoghurt, stirring until combined. Pour into the flour mix and stir together until you have a rough ball of dough. Tip on to a floured baking sheet and pat into a smooth ball with your hands. Flatten slightly, then cut a deep cross shape on top.

When the oven is running at about 180–200°C (350–400°F), slide the baking sheet in, shut the door and bake for about 25 minutes – rotating the sheet halfway through for an even bake. The cheese makes this a tricky candidate for bare baking, so it's best left on the tray. Allow to cool a little before eating, and serve in wedges, with plenty of butter.

AND ANOTHER THING...

● For a slightly sweet spicy soda bread, leave out the cheese and herbs and in their place add a good handful of raisins and a teaspoon of mixed spice. Or try dried cranberries and ground ginger.
● Use a different cheese and vary the herbs, depending on what you have lying around.
● Keep it super simple and add nothing extra at all!

CUMIN AND SMOKED PAPRIKA SHORTBREAD

These savoury shortbread biscuits make an awesome, moreish little snack and are just perfect with a glass of wine while you wait for your oven to get to pizza temperature. Best of all, you can make the shortbread whenever you like, freeze the dough in a cylinder and just slice off bits when you want to cook a few. (Pictured on page 69, right.)

200–220°C (400–425°F)
MAKES LOTS! ABOUT 40 LITTLE NIBBLY BISCUITS

150g (1¼ cups) plain
    (all-purpose) flour
50g (½ cup) cornflour (cornstarch)
1 tbsp cumin seeds
1 heaped tsp smoked paprika
½ tsp salt
150g (¾ cup) cold butter, diced
100g (¾ cup) extra mature Cheddar,
    grated
2 tbsp ice-cold water

You need the oven to be about 200–220°C (400–425°F) for these biscuits. These quick cooking biscuits are a great bar snack and a good thing to slide into the oven while it's coming up to a hotter pizza temperature. Just keep a close eye on them, rotating the tin frequently so they cook evenly.

Put the flour and cornflour into a mixing bowl and stir in the cumin seeds, paprika and salt. Add the diced butter and rub between your fingers and thumbs, as if you were making pastry, until you have fine crumbs. Alternatively you can pulse in a food processor, taking care not to overwork otherwise the shortbread will be tough rather than tender.

Add the cheese and stir through, or pulse briefly if you are using a food processor. Then add just enough ice-cold water to bring it together into a crumbly ball. Tip it on to a sheet of clingfilm and shape into a long thin log about 2½cm (1in) in diameter, cutting into two lengths if it's too unwieldy. Wrap tightly in clingfilm and freeze until pretty much solid. The shortbread will also keep in the freezer for 3 months, provided it's well wrapped.

When you are ready to bake, remove the log, unwrap on a chopping board and use a sharp serrated breadknife to carve off approximately 5mm (½in) discs, laying them on a baking sheet as you go. Slide the baking sheet into the oven and cook for about 10–12 minutes, until the biscuits are golden. Rotate once or twice to make sure they cook evenly. They will still be a touch soft when you take them out of the oven, but they will crisp up as they cool (if you can wait that long . . .).

AND ANOTHER THING...

• **Parmesan, black olive and anchovy** – sub the Cheddar and spices with 75g (¾ cup) of grated Parmesan, 50g (½ cup) of finely chopped pitted black olives and 2 tablespoons of finely chopped anchovy fillets, along with the chopped needles picked from a few sprigs of fresh rosemary.

• **Blue cheese and nuts** – sub the Cheddar with 100g (¾ cup) of crumbled blue cheese (I like to use a creamy Cashel Blue) and 50g (½ cup) of finely chopped hazelnuts or walnuts.

WALNUT AND BLACK PEPPER 'LEAF BREAD' WITH BAKED CAMEMBERT

The proper name for this multi-lobed bread is 'fougasse', but my daughter said it looked like a leaf, and so leaf bread it has become. Whatever you call it, it is delicious – the shape of the bread gives you maximum crust, which is exactly what you want to scoop up the oozing cheese. Inspiration for this bread came from the brilliant Chez Panisse Menu cookbook by Alice Waters. Alice's recipe is rather more complex and she, of course, calls it by its proper name . . .

200–210°C (400–410°F)
MAKES ONE LARGE FLAT LOAF, SERVING ABOUT 4 AS STARTER OR AS PART OF A TAPAS MEAL

300g (2¼ cups) strong white
  bread flour
1 tsp freshly ground black pepper
½ tsp instant yeast
½ tsp fine salt
100g (1 cup) walnuts
200ml (¾ cup) hand-hot water
olive oil, for kneading and drizzling

For the Camembert
1 whole ripe Camembert
1 clove of garlic, finely sliced
a sprig of fresh rosemary, needles
  picked
2 tbsp dry sherry (use dry
  white vermouth or white wine
  if you prefer)
sea salt flakes and freshly ground
  black pepper

You need an even baking temperature of around 200°C (400°F) for this bread. Because it is thin it cooks pretty fast, so you can cook it with a little live flame with the door ajar, or you can cook with the glowing embers and the door shut. It's quite a forgiving kind of bread.

Put the flour, black pepper, yeast and salt into a mixing bowl and stir well to mix. Whizz the walnuts in a food processor until they are coarsely ground, or chop very finely with a sharp knife. Stir into the flour mix. Pour in the warm water and bring the dough together with a wooden spoon until it forms a rough ball. Set aside for 10 minutes for the flour to hydrate.

Lightly oil the worktop and tip the dough on to it. Scrape any bits of flour from the bowl, and drizzle the inside with a little oil, using your hands to spread it all over. With oiled hands, very lightly knead the dough for just 10 seconds, with one pull per second. Put back into the bowl, cover and set aside for 10 minutes. Repeat this 10-second knead and 10-minute rest twice more. Put the dough back into the bowl, cover and leave until risen by a good 50 per cent, which will take an hour or so.

Once the dough has risen, lightly flour the worktop and scrape the dough on to it. Using floured hands, gently flatten and pat the dough into an oval that's about two-thirds the size of your wooden peel. Lift on to a lightly floured wooden peel and use a really sharp knife to cut diagonal slashes on one side of the loaf from the middle to nearly the edge, opening up the gaps so it looks like a large tropical leaf. Repeat on the other side, then set aside to prove for another 30 minutes.

Meanwhile, get the Camembert ready for baking. Unwrap the cheese and place it in a small heatproof dish – I use a shallow enamel bowl, but any small baking dish would be fine. Use a small sharp knife to pierce a dozen slits in the top, and into these press slivers of garlic and bits of rosemary. Drizzle over the sherry and season with salt and pepper.

Immediately before baking, drizzle the bread with a little oil and sprinkle over some sea salt flakes. Slide the loaf into the hot oven and bake for 15 minutes. After that time, slide the dish of cheese alongside, and rotate the bread if necessary to make sure it's cooking evenly. Bake both for another 10–15 minutes, until the cheese is oozing and the bread is crisp.

Serve immediately, while hot.

WOOD-FIRED CREAM TEA WITH ROAST RASPBERRY JAM

A small cook's confession . . . I had originally intended this recipe to be wood-fired crumpets, to go with the baked raspberry jam, but as it turns out I just couldn't make a crumpet that tasted better than one I could buy, and there was a considerable amount of faff trying. However, as a Cornish girl who grew up in Devon, I absolutely knew I could get delicious scones on the table without any fuss whatsoever, and so here it is, an easy-peasy, wood-fired cream tea. I always make one big scone, scored into wedges so it looks like a flower, as it's infinitely more straightforward than cutting out rounds and re-rolling the scraps. The less you handle a scone the lighter it will be.

The jam is foolproof, just two ingredients and 20 minutes of your time and it's done. Just make sure you cook it in a deep saucepan, so it doesn't bubble up all over your oven floor. I made plenty, a little more than we could eat with the scones, as I knew it would get used up, but it's an easy recipe to adjust – just use equal quantities of fruit to sugar. It will keep in the fridge for a couple of weeks.

240–250°C (460–480°F)
MAKES 8 WEDGES OF SCONE, SERVING 4–6

For the oven-roast raspberry jam
350g (2⅔ cups) frozen raspberries
350g (1¾ cups) caster (superfine) sugar

For the scones
450g (3¼ cups) self-raising flour, plus a little extra for dusting
2 tbsp caster (superfine) sugar
½ tsp salt
75g (⅓ cup) butter, diced into cubes
300ml (1¼ cups) milk
clotted cream, to serve

You need a good hot baking temperature for this recipe, with no live flame, as you cook with the door shut.

Put the raspberries into a sturdy deep saucepan. Sprinkle over the sugar and toss to coat. Slide the jam pan into the oven and cook for 20 minutes, stirring a couple of times to mix the sugar in as it melts. Remove from the oven, allow to cool a little and transfer to a bowl.

Once the jam is cooking, begin the scones. Weigh the flour into a mixing bowl and stir in the sugar and salt. Add the cubes of butter and rub between fingers and thumbs until it is evenly blended. Pour in the milk and use a tablespoon to fold gently together until you have a dough. Take care not to over-mix, and stop as soon as the flour is combined with the milk.

Tip on to a lightly floured worktop and pat into a circle of about 16–18cm (6¼–7in) in diameter and 4cm (1½in) thick. Lift on to a floured baking sheet and lightly dust the top with flour. Use a sharp knife to cut all the way through into 8 wedges, leaving them together in a round shape, like cutting a cake.

Slide into the hot oven and bake for about 20–25 minutes, checking halfway through cooking and rotating the tin to make sure it is cooking evenly. Allow to cool a little before serving.

PASTÉIS DE NATA

The secret to making good pastéis de nata is a very high heat, something that's not easy to achieve in a domestic oven but is blissfully simple in a wood-fired one. Begin the pastry and custard several hours or even a couple of days before you want to bake, as they both need plenty of time for chilling.

250–260°C (480–500°F)
MAKES 12

For the pastry
150g (1 cup) plain (all-purpose) flour, plus more for rolling
75ml (¼ cup) cold water
150g (¾ cup) butter, softened to an easy spreading consistency

For the custard
3 egg yolks
1 whole egg
175g (1 cup) caster (superfine) sugar
25g (1 tbsp) plain (all-purpose) flour
1 tsp vanilla extract
300ml (1¼ cups) milk

You also need a 12-hole muffin tin.

The oven needs to be fired up to a good steady baking temperature of about 250–260°C (480–500°F). As this recipe gets cooked with the door closed, there shouldn't be any live flames.

Put the flour into a mixing bowl and add the cold water, stirring with a spoon to bring it together. Tip it on to a worktop and knead briefly until you have a smooth-ish dough. Wrap in clingfilm and chill for 30 minutes.

On a lightly floured worktop, pat the chilled dough into a rough rectangle. Roll it out into a large rectangle about 5mm (¼in) thick, with the shortest edge nearest your body. Spread about a third of the butter all over the pastry, going nearly to the edges. Fold the bottom third of the pastry up and over to the middle, then fold the top third up and down over the top, like folding a letter to go in an envelope. Wrap in clingfilm and chill for another 30 minutes. After 30 minutes, lay the chilled dough 90° from where you finished rolling it, so the folds run top to bottom rather than right to left. Roll it out again into a large rectangle, spread with another third of the soft butter and fold again, letter-style. Wrap and chill for another 30 minutes. Repeat this process once more, again starting at 90° from where you finished on the previous roll. Wrap and chill for 30 minutes again.

Remove from the fridge and roll out one last time, into a rectangle 5mm (¼in) thick, then roll up tightly like a snake. Wrap and chill for another 30 minutes. At this point you can freeze the pastry for up to 3 months.

To make the custard, put the egg yolks, whole egg, sugar, flour and vanilla into a mixing bowl. Use an electric whisk to beat together for 2–3 minutes, until thick, pale and creamy.

Pour the milk into a small heavy-based pan and set over a medium heat. Bring up to boiling point, then remove from the heat and pour into the egg and sugar mixture. Whisk until thoroughly combined, then pour into a jug. Cover the surface with a bit of clingfilm, pressed close to it so a skin doesn't form, and set aside to cool completely. At this point you can put it into the fridge until you are ready to bake – it will be fine for up to 3 days.

Take the roll of pastry and trim off the ends neatly, then cut into 12 even-sized discs. Press a disc into a muffin-tin hole, easing the pastry down to the bottom and pressing it up the sides so it comes all the way to the top. You want the pastry to be an even thickness all over. Repeat with the remaining pastry discs. Chill in the fridge for another 30 minutes.

When you are ready to cook, take the tray of pastry cases and the jug of custard to the oven. Fill the pastry cases with the custard – they should be pretty full. Carefully slide the muffin tray into the oven and shut the door. After 10–12 minutes, rotate the tray to make sure the tarts are cooking evenly, then cook for another 10 minutes or so. They are ready when the pastry is crisp and the tops have lovely deep caramelized patches all over.

Allow to cool a little, then ease them out of the tin using a table knife. Eat warm or at room temperature. Best eaten on the day they were made.

FIG, HONEY AND BRANDY CLAFOUTIS

Clafoutis is a creamy, dreamy pudding with a tongue-twister of name. It's like a dense egg custard crossed with a sweet Yorkshire pudding, managing at the same time to be unctuous in the middle and puffy as a cloud at the edges. Traditionally made with cherries – and indeed this is lovely too (see the flavour variations below) – here I have made it with plump fresh figs that have been liberally doused in brandy. You could serve it with a drizzle of thick cream, but I think it's pretty much perfect just as it is.

220–240°C (425–460°F)
SERVES ABOUT 6

60g (about ¼ cup) melted butter
8 large ripe figs (about 450g/1lb)
3 tbsp brandy
75g (¾ cup) plain (all-purpose) flour
3 eggs
250ml (1 cup) milk
100ml (⅓ cup) double (heavy) cream
4 tbsp runny honey
1 tsp vanilla extract
icing (confectioners') sugar,
   to dust

You also need a 25–26cm (10–10½in) diameter ceramic dish or metal tin to cook the clafoutis in – I use a deep ovenproof frying pan, i.e. one with no plastic handles.

The oven needs to be running at a good hot baking temperature of about 220–240°C (425–460°F), with no live flame, so you can shut the door.

Brush a little of the melted butter around the inside of your chosen pan, and reserve the rest for the batter.

Slice the figs through in a cross shape, cutting from the top about three-quarters of the way down to the base. Squeeze the figs a little to open them out, and arrange them in the pan, well spaced out. Drizzle the brandy into the cuts in the figs and set aside.

To make the batter, put the flour into a mixing bowl. Make a well in the middle and crack in the eggs. Gently pour in the milk, followed by the cream and reserved melted butter, whisking all the time to make a smooth batter. Add the honey and vanilla and whisk once more until combined. Set aside to rest for a few minutes, or up to an hour or two in the fridge.

When you are ready to cook, give the batter a little whisk to mix it once more, then pour it around the brandy-soaked figs. Slide the dish into the oven, shut the door, and bake for about 25–35 minutes, depending on the heat. The clafoutis is ready when it's puffed up and golden, with just a little bit of a wobble in the centre. If it starts to colour too much on top, move it to a cooler part of the oven, or cover loosely with foil.

Leave the clafoutis to cool to the warm side of room temperature (it will deflate and settle a little), and dust with icing sugar just before serving. Serve scooped into bowls, with a little cream poured over if you fancy.

AND ANOTHER THING...

• Any stone fruits – quartered plums, apricots, greengages – are great too. Use slightly more than the weight of the figs, to take account for the stones that need removing.
• Blackberries, raspberries and blueberries are all lovely too – try matching the fruit to various fruit liqueurs, or simply omit the booze for a child-friendly version.

PEAR, GINGER AND CHOCOLATE CRUMBLE

The steady all-round heat from a well-insulated wood-fired oven makes a legendary crumble – the bottom heat from the oven base softening your chosen fruit beautifully, while the radiant heat from the oven walls crisps up the topping a treat. Use a really light touch when scattering the crumble topping over the fruit, resisting the urge to level or press it down too much. Lots of little air gaps means the crumble will bake with a lovely crisp, open texture. This recipe uses a rather classic combination of pears, chocolate and ginger, but feel free to ring the changes with whatever fruit takes your fancy.

190–200°C (375–400°F)
SERVES ABOUT 6

For the filling

850–950g (1lb 12oz–2lb 2oz) ripe Conference pears (about 4 large, 6 medium)

75g (½ cup) stem ginger, finely chopped, plus 4 tbsp syrup from the jar

100g (3½oz) dark chocolate, broken into squares

For the crumble

50g (about ½ cup) hazelnuts

200g (1½ cups) plain (all-purpose) flour

125g (just over ½ cup) butter, diced into 1cm (½in) cubes

75g (⅓ cup) caster (superfine) sugar

You need the oven to be running at about 190–200°C (375–400°F), with no live flame.

Peel the pears, quarter them and remove the core. Cut each quarter in half and put them in a 22–24cm (8½–9½in) round baking dish. Scatter over the chopped ginger and spoon in the syrup, stirring well to coat the pieces of pear. Tuck in the squares of chocolate, and set aside. You can assemble the filling a couple of hours before you want to cook, if you want to get ahead.

To make the crumble, put the hazelnuts into a food processor and pulse a few times to chop coarsely. Tip in the flour, add the cubes of butter, and pulse again until the mix looks like coarse, lumpy breadcrumbs. Finally add the sugar and pulse a few more times until just combined. Don't over-process or the crumble will be heavy. You can also make the crumble by hand, by rubbing the butter and flour together between fingers and thumbs, then mixing in the finely chopped hazelnuts and sugar. Set aside until you are ready to bake.

When the oven is at temperature and you are ready to bake, lightly scatter the crumble over the pears without pressing or patting it down too much.

Rest the dish on a baking tray and slide it into the hot oven. Shut the door and bake for about 40 minutes, until the top is crisp and golden and the filling is starting to bubble up around the edges.

AND ANOTHER THING...

• Try swapping the fruit for whatever is ripe and seasonal. The stem ginger is optional – it goes well with plums, greengages and rhubarb, perhaps not quite so well with apples.

• The nuts add an optional crunch that I love, but leave them out if you prefer, or swap for another type of nut – walnuts, almonds, pecans are all good crumble partners.

PRUNE, APRICOT AND EARL GREY TEA BREAD

This couldn't be an easier bake, but you do need to give the fruit plenty of time for soaking – at least 12 hours, ideally 24. It's just the sort of simple, not-too-sweet cake I relish with a cuppa in the afternoon, and it makes a pretty decent breakfast on the move too. All in all a useful sort of cake to have kicking about, and one that keeps well in an airtight tin, a good 5–7 days or so. A slick of butter on each slice is optional, but I always would – there being no added fat in the cake itself, it feels entirely justified.

190–200°C (375–400°F)
MAKES ONE LOAF CAKE

2 Earl Grey teabags
150g (1¼ cups) prunes, chopped
150g (1¼ cups) dried apricots, chopped
100g (½ cup) dark brown sugar
2 eggs
250g (2 cups) self-raising (self-rising) flour

You also need a 900g (2lb) loaf tin.

You need the oven to be running at around 190–200°C (375–400°F), with no live flame.

Put the teabags into a heatproof measuring jug and pour over 250ml (1 cup) of boiling water. Leave to brew for a good 5 minutes, then remove the tea bags. Put the prunes, apricots and sugar into a mixing bowl and pour over the hot tea. Cover and leave to sit overnight, for at least 12 hours, or up to 24 if you can.

The next day, when you are ready to bake, grease your loaf tin and line it with baking paper.

Crack the eggs into the bowl of soaked fruit, and beat together to mix. Add the flour and stir thoroughly, until just combined, then pour into the prepared loaf tin.

Set the tin on a baking sheet so that it's easier to manoeuvre in and out of the oven, and slide it into the oven, shutting the door. Leave to bake for about 40–45 minutes, checking once or twice and rotating the tray to make sure the tea bread is cooking evenly. It is cooked when a metal skewer inserted into the centre comes out clean. If the top is browning too much, cover loosely with a double layer of foil and continue baking.

Remove from the oven and allow to cool in the tin for a few minutes, then run a table knife around the edge and invert on to a cooling rack.

Serve while still warm or at room temperature, spread with a little butter if you like.

AND ANOTHER THING...

• Instead of a half and half mix of prunes and apricots, use just one or the other.
• In fact . . . use any dried fruit you fancy! Raisins, sultanas, dates and cranberries are all lovely.
• Add a little chopped mixed peel along with the fruit.

ORANGE BLOSSOM-SCENTED RICE PUDDING WITH ROAST RHUBARB

Rice pudding gets something of a bad rap, its reputation rather tarnished by mediocre school dinners of old, but properly done it is a thing of luscious beauty. As a bonus, it's also one of the simplest puddings you can ever make – you pretty much chuck it all in a pot and shove it in the oven. Here I serve it with rhubarb that has been roasted with orange, as I love the sharp contrast between fruit and cream. My preference, just as with the clafoutis on page 116, is to leave the cooked pud to settle a while and serve it on the warm side of room temperature. I just think it's more flavoursome that way, but it's also pretty good straight from the fridge for an indulgent breakfast.

180–210°C (350–410°F)
SERVES 4–6

a little butter, for greasing the dish
750ml (3¼ cups) milk
250ml (1 cup) double (heavy) cream
150g ¾ cup) pudding rice
75g (⅓ cup) caster (superfine) sugar
1–2 tbsp orange blossom water,
  to taste

For the rhubarb
400g (14oz) rhubarb, washed and
  cut into 4cm (1½in) lengths
zest and juice of 1 large orange
4 tbsp granulated sugar

You also need a ceramic baking dish of about 1.5 litres (2¾ pints) capacity.

The oven needs to be running at a baking temperature of 180–210°C (350–410°F), with no live flames, so you can shut the door. Temperature here is not critical – if it's a little hot it will cook quicker, but you may need to cover the top loosely with foil if it starts to burn.

Grease the inside of the baking dish with a little butter. Pour in the milk and cream, then add the rice, sugar and orange blossom water. Give everything a little stir. Slide the dish into the oven, shut the door, and leave to bake for 1½ hours.

Meanwhile, spread the rhubarb in a snug single layer in a roasting tin or dish. Add the zest and juice of the orange, along with the sugar, and toss to mix.

Once the rice has been in the oven for 45 minutes, check to make sure the top isn't colouring too much – if it is, cover with foil and return it to the oven. Slide the rhubarb into the oven alongside the rice and shut the door again. Leave both to bake for another 45 minutes, until the rhubarb is tender and a touch caramelized around the edges. The rice pudding is cooked when the rice is tender – the creamy sauce will still be a little liquid, but it will thicken more as it cools.

Leave to cool a little before serving, as I think it is best eaten warm rather than piping hot. Serve scooped into bowls, with the rhubarb and juice spooned over the top.

AND ANOTHER THING...

• Swap the orange blossom water for rosewater or vanilla extract.
• Keep the rice simple with just milk, cream and sugar, and grate over plenty of nutmeg just before you bake.
• If rhubarb is not your thing, try the rice pudding with one of the roast fruit ideas on page 86.

NECTARINE, RASPBERRY AND ALMOND UPSIDE-DOWN CAKE

My very favourite cakes are a combination of buttery, almondy sponge with some sort of fruit, and this is a fantastic example. I think of it more as a pudding cake rather than a teatime treat, and it's perfect served with a big dollop of crème fraîche on top. The caramel topping and fruit can be prepared well ahead of time, so all you need to do is whip up the sponge just before baking.

170–200°C (325–400°F)
MAKES 1 CAKE, SERVING ABOUT 6 FOR PUDDING

225g (1 cup) butter
75g (⅓ cup) soft brown sugar
3 large ripe nectarines, cut into
    thick wedges
150g (1 cup) raspberries
125g (⅔ cup) caster (superfine)
    sugar
2 eggs
75g (¾ cup) self-raising flour
75g (¾ cup) ground almonds
2 tbsp milk

You also need a deep ovenproof (i.e. no plastic handles) frying pan about 26cm (10½in) in diameter.

The oven needs to be running at between 170–200°C (325–400°F) for this cake, the cooking times varying a little depending on the heat, and the door needs to be shut, so no live flames.

Put a third of the butter and all the brown sugar into the frying pan and set over a medium heat on the hob. Allow to melt and bubble, stirring occasionally, until it forms a deep, dark caramel sauce. Turn off the heat and set aside to cool.

Once the sauce is cold, arrange the nectarine slices, cut side down, in the pan. Tuck the raspberries, hole side up, into the gaps, so you have a snugly packed layer of fruit that covers the whole base. You can be as neat or as random as you like when arranging your fruit – it's your call. Set the pan aside until you are ready to bake the cake – it will sit happily for a few hours in the fridge if you want to get ahead.

When you are ready to bake, cream together the caster sugar and the rest of the butter until light and fluffy, either with an electric whisk or a free-standing food mixer. Add the eggs, one at a time, beating well after each addition. Finally add the flour, ground almonds and milk and beat until smooth.

Pour the sponge batter over the prepared fruit, levelling it to the edges with a table knife. Slide the pan into the oven, shut the door, and bake until the top of the cake is golden and the sponge is cooked through – a metal skewer inserted into the sponge should come out clean. This will take around 25 minutes at 180–190°C (350–375°F), and more like about 30–35 minutes if the temperature is lower. Check the sponge halfway through cooking and rotate the pan to make sure it cooks evenly. If your oven is running quite hot and it's browning too fast, move it to a cooler part of the oven or cover the top loosely with foil.

Remove from the oven and allow to cool in the pan for 15 minutes, then run a knife around the edge and invert on to a serving plate.

AND ANOTHER THING...

● Use wedges of eating apple as the fruit layer – you will need 2 or 3 apples, peeled, cored and cut into thick wedges – and add a teaspoon of ground cinnamon or mixed spice to the sponge mix.
● Go retro and make the original pineapple upside-down cake – rings of pineapple canned in juice are a must, and pop a glacé cherry into each pineapple hole to achieve that genuine old-school look.

FLAPJACK

In my world, flapjack should be a bit crunchy round the edges. I like a little bit of snap when I bite into it – that's how Mum made it when we were kids and that's how I make it for my kids now. If you, like I know many people do, prefer it softer and more chewy, it's an easy thing to do – simply bake it in a smaller, deeper tin for slightly less time. With flapjack, simplicity always works best for me – the marriage of butter, sugar, syrup and oats is pretty much perfect as it is – but there are a few flavour suggestions below if you want to pimp your bake. Using a mix of regular and jumbo oats ups the crunch and texture a little.

170–200°C (325–400°F)
MAKES ABOUT 16 PIECES

250g (1½ cups) butter
250g (¾ cup) golden syrup
100g (½ cup) soft brown sugar
500g (3¾ cups) rolled oats
    (or a mix of rolled oats and
    whole jumbo oats, as you like)

You also need a baking tin – either about 28cm (11in) square and 1cm (½in) deep for thin crisp flapjack, or about 23cm (9in) square and 3–4cm (1¼–1½in) deep for a thicker, softer bake. Line it with baking paper to help you lift the flapjack out of the tin.

When you are ready to bake you want your oven to be running at 170–200°C (325–400°F). The exact temperature isn't vital, the flapjack will simply take more or less time to cook.

Put the butter, syrup and sugar into a small heavy-based pan and set over a medium heat to melt together. If you are using syrup from a squeezy bottle, it's easy to weigh it into the pan. If it's from a traditional tin, heat up a tablespoon in a jug of boiling water for a few seconds and use the hot spoon to measure out the syrup – you'll save yourself a lot of sticky effort, as it will slide from the spoon effortlessly.

Meanwhile, put the oats into a mixing bowl, stirring them together if you are using both sizes. Pour over the hot butter, syrup and sugar mixture and stir well. Spoon into your chosen tin, levelling firmly with the back of a tablespoon. Set aside until you are ready to bake – the uncooked flapjack will keep very happily for several hours, covered, on the worktop.

When you are ready to cook, slide it into the oven and cook until deep golden brown – this will take 20–30 minutes, depending on the heat you give it and the finished texture you are after. The flapjack will still feel soft to touch when hot, but it will firm as it cools. When it's cool but not yet cold, use a small sharp knife to score it through into 16 even-ish pieces. Once cold, store in an airtight tin.

AND ANOTHER THING...

With all of these, simply stir through once everything else is mixed:
- A handful or two of dried fruit – sultanas, raisins, cranberries, chopped apricots or prunes.
- A handful of desiccated coconut.
- A handful of chopped nuts or seeds.
- Some chocolate chips – white, plain or milk.
- Some chopped stem ginger or a few spoons of chunky marmalade.

M'HANNCHA (SNAKE CAKE)

Crispy pastry, rolled around rosewater-scented frangipane and coiled around and around until it looks positively snake-like, m'hanncha is a fab thing to bake for sharing with a crowd – it's great served with coffee at the end of a meal. It also keeps really well and you can just cut off a little (or a large) piece of the coil whenever you like. This traditional northern Moroccan dessert is usually made with warka (or brick) pastry but here I've made it with the infinitely easier to source filo.

160–180°C (325–350°F)
MAKES 1 LARGE CAKE, SERVING 8–10

200g (1 cup) butter, diced
250g (2 cups) icing (confectioners')
  sugar, plus a little for dusting
400g (4 cups) ground almonds
2 eggs
1–3 tbsp rosewater, to taste
125g (1 cup) dried apricots, finely
  chopped
100g (¾ cup) pistachios, chopped
220–250g (8–9oz) pack of filo
  (phyllo) pastry
50g (¼ cup) melted butter, to brush

You also need a deep 23cm (9in)
round springform tin, lined on the
base with baking paper and the
base and sides well greased with
butter.

Put the butter into a free-standing food mixer (or use a roomy bowl and an electric whisk) and beat with the paddle attachment until softened. Add the icing sugar and beat very slowly until combined so it doesn't shower you in sugar-dust, then turn the speed up and beat for a couple of minutes until light and fluffy. Add the ground almonds and eggs and beat once more until you have a smooth, creamy paste. Now add the rosewater – start with a tablespoon, beating well to mix, and increase until you are happy with the flavour. Finally, fold in all the apricots and most of the pistachios, reserving a few to garnish. Chill in the fridge for a couple of hours so it's firm.

When you are ready to assemble the cake – and it can be done a few hours before baking – unroll the filo and place one sheet on a clear worktop. Cover the rest with a damp tea towel to stop it drying out.

Brush the filo all over with a little butter, then fold in half to create a double thickness. Spoon a little of the filling in a line along the side closest to you, leaving a couple of centimetres (an inch or so) clear at either end. Shape the filling into a log about 2cm (¾in) in diameter. Fold over the bare ends of the filo, and roll it up so you have a neat cylinder. Then begin to coil this cylinder around on itself like a snail shell (or indeed a sleeping snake!); it may crack a little – this is the hardest section to coil, as the angles are tightest. Lift into the centre of the springform tin. Patch any cracks with little bits of filo, stuck on with melted butter.

For the next part of the snake, which will be easier to coil, use two sheets of filo, again covering the rest of the pack to prevent it drying out. Lay one sheet on top of the other, buttering in between, to make a double sheet, and lay a long log of filling along the edge nearest to you, as before, folding and rolling it up into a tight cylinder. Lay one end of the cylinder butted up tight to where the first coil finished, and continue to coil it around to make your snake bigger. Once again, patch any cracks with extra filo and melted butter. Repeat this process until you have used all the filling. Brush all over with butter and set aside until you are ready to bake.

Once you are ready to cook, slide the tin into the oven, shut the door and cook for about 45 minutes, until the m'hanncha is golden brown and crispy, checking and rotating the tin once or twice to make sure it's cooking evenly. Cover the top loosely with foil if it's getting too dark – if your oven is running a bit hot, it may colour too quickly. Leave to cool to room temperature, then run a table knife around the edge to release the springform. Scatter over the remaining pistachios and dust liberally with icing sugar before serving. To serve, break off little pieces of the coils, working from the outside in.

AND ANOTHER THING...

• Swap the rosewater for orange flower water.
• Swap the apricots for chopped dates or candied mixed peel.
• Swap the pistachios for another chopped nut – walnuts or hazelnuts are great.

ROAST PUMPKIN AND MASCARPONE PEARL BARLEY ORZOTTO

Quite simply, orzotto is a risotto made from pearl barley rather than rice, and I have to say I almost prefer it – the grains retain a little of their chewy texture, giving the dish a bit more substance. You do need to add something in the way of creaminess, as pearl barley doesn't have the starch that rice does. In this recipe, that comes from a generous helping of mascarpone cheese, but you could use something like ripe melting Gorgonzola instead. Roasting the pumpkin in the wood oven really intensifies the flavour, and it's well worth taking the time to make sure it has lots of good caramelized edges to it before you add the stock.

230–240°C (450–460°F)
SERVES 4

1.1–1.2kg (2lb 6oz– 2lb 10oz)
    pumpkin or squash, peeled
    and cut into 2cm (¾in) chunks
2 tbsp olive oil
a few sprigs of fresh thyme,
    or 1 tsp dried thyme
2 red onions, chopped
3 cloves of garlic, chopped
300g (1½ cups) pearl barley
1 litre (1¾ pints) vegetable or
    chicken stock
250g (1¼ cups) mascarpone
salt and freshly ground black
    pepper

To serve
a good handful of basil, finely
    shredded
Parmesan shavings

Put the pumpkin into a large, deep overproof frying pan. Pour over the olive oil, tuck in the thyme, and season generously with salt and pepper, tossing well to mix. Slide the pan into the hot oven and roast for 15 minutes, then take the pan from the fire and add the onions, stirring well to mix. Slide the pan back into the oven for another 20 minutes, stirring once or twice to make sure it is all cooking evenly. Remove the pan once more and stir in the garlic, then slide back in and cook for 5 minutes.

Stir in the pearl barley and pour in the stock, again stirring so it's all really well mixed. Slide back into the oven and cook for 30 minutes, stirring a couple of times. After this time, taste the barley – it should be cooked but still have a little bite to it. If it's still a touch hard, keep cooking for another few minutes, adding a splash of water if it's becoming a bit dry.

Lastly, add the mascarpone and lightly fold in, then return the pan to the oven to heat through for a final 5 minutes. Don't over-mix – it's really delicious to come across little pockets of molten creamy cheese as you eat.

To serve, spoon into warmed bowls and scatter over plenty of basil and Parmesan. Eat while piping hot.

ROAST CAULIFLOWER SFORMATO

Originating from Italy, a sformato is like a cross between a dense soufflé and a pastry-less quiche. All you need to serve it with is a big salad, and you have a delicious main meal. If there is a trick to pass on to maximize flavour, it is to roast the vegetables thoroughly, so they are really nicely caramelized, and to be fairly heavy-handed with the seasoning – so don't stint on the herbs and spices, or the salt and pepper.

220–270°C (425–520°F)
SERVES 4–6

1 large cauliflower (about 1.2kg/2½lb), chopped into florets
1 large onion, finely chopped
3 tbsp olive oil, plus a little for greasing the tin
a small bunch of fresh sage, leaves roughly chopped
80g (⅓ cup) butter
80g (¾ cup) plain (all-purpose) flour
800ml (3⅓ cups) milk
75g (1 cup) freshly grated Parmesan
2 tsp English or Dijon mustard
5 large eggs
salt and freshly ground black pepper

You also need a springform tin 6cm (2½in) deep, 23cm (9in) in diameter, lined with baking paper and brushed with a little olive oil.

AND ANOTHER THING...

• Swap the cauliflower for the same weight of carrots, chopped into 3–4cm (1¼–1½in) chunks. Season them with a tablespoon of cumin seeds rather than the sage, and fold through a loose handful of chopped coriander.
• Add the same weight of chopped butternut squash, seasoning with crushed coriander seeds and a few dried chilli flakes rather than the sage. Add a handful of chopped flat-leaf parsley to the sauce.

You need the oven to be at a high roasting temperature of about 260–270°C (500–520°F) at the start of this recipe, and then to bake the sformato it needs to be a little lower, about 220–230°C (425–450°F).

Tip the cauliflower and onion into a large roasting tin, drizzle over the oil, sprinkle on the sage and season well with salt and freshly ground black pepper. Toss well to mix. Slide the tin into the oven, at about 260°C (500°F), and roast for 35–40 minutes with the door on and slightly ajar, removing and stirring once or twice to make sure the cauliflower is cooking evenly. When it's cooked it will be tender with just a touch of bite, and the edges will be lightly caramelized.

Meanwhile, on the hob in the kitchen, melt the butter in a large saucepan and stir in the flour to form a roux. Gradually pour in the milk, whisking constantly, then bring to the boil to allow the sauce to thicken. Let it bubble away, stirring frequently, for 5–8 minutes, to cook the flour. Turn off the heat, then stir in the cheese, mustard and a grind of pepper – you may want to add a little salt too, but bear in mind the cauliflower is seasoned, so don't overdo it. Crack in the eggs and beat together, making sure they are really well mixed in. Set aside until the cauliflower is ready.

Once the cauliflower is cooked, remove it from the oven. At the same time, check the temperature of your oven floor – you want it to be about 220–230°C (425–450°F). If it's at the right temperature, shut the oven door to keep the heat in. If it's too hot, leave the door off and allow it to cool a little.

Break up the cauliflower a little, using a metal spoon, so you have some smaller pieces and some larger pieces. Tip it into the sauce, along with the onions and bits of crisp sage, and fold together. Once the oven is at the right temperature, pour the mixture into the springform tin and slide it into the oven. Bake for 45–50 minutes, until a skewer inserted into the centre comes out just about clean. It will be deep golden brown, with a very slight wobble to the centre. Check halfway through, rotating the tin if necessary to make sure it's cooking evenly, and cover the top loosely with foil if it's getting too brown.

Allow to cool in the tin for 10 minutes, then slide a knife around the edge and release the springform. Cut into wedges, and serve with a tomato salad.

NEWSPAPER-BAKED SALMON WITH WINTER-SPICED ONION AND PINE NUT STUFFING

Cooking a large piece of salmon feels like a festive treat, and this is exactly the sort of thing I might make for a Christmas Eve feast, served with dauphinoise potatoes (see page 151) and some crisp watercress or steamed purple sprouting broccoli. The spicing is subtle, a very gentle nod to the season, while the abundant parsley and pine nuts feel just a touch Middle Eastern. I like to use a couple of 1kg (2lb 4oz) salmon fillets, with the stuffing sandwiched between them for ease of 'carving', and I make sure my fishmonger cuts them so they are the same size and fit together neatly. However, you could also adapt this recipe to use a 2kg (4lb 8oz) whole salmon if you like, using the stuffing in the gut cavity – the cooking time should be pretty similar.

200–230°C (400–450°F)
SERVES ABOUT 8

2 x 1kg (2lb 4oz) salmon side fillets
1 lemon, cut into wedges, to serve

For the stuffing
100g (½ cup) pine nuts
1 tbsp olive oil
25g (2 tbsp) butter
3 red onions, sliced
½ tsp ground cinnamon
½ tsp ground mace
a pinch of ground cloves or ½ tsp
   whole cloves
a large bunch of fresh
   parsley, chopped
salt and freshly ground black
   pepper

You also need baking paper, a whole newspaper and some string to tie it up.

You need the oven to be running at around 200–230°C (400–450°F), with not much flame and plenty of glowing embers so you can roast with the door ajar.

Begin by making the stuffing. You can do this several hours in advance if you want to get ahead. Set a large frying pan over a high heat, tip in the pine nuts, and let them toast to a golden brown. Transfer to a bowl and set aside.

Reduce the heat under the pan to low and add the olive oil and butter, allowing the butter to melt for a few seconds. Stir in the onions and leave to cook for a good 30–40 minutes, until really soft and caramelized. Halfway through, stir in the cinnamon, mace and cloves, and season with a little salt and pepper. Once the onions are cooked, turn off the heat and stir in the parsley and the toasted pine nuts. Transfer to a bowl and leave to cool.

When you are ready to cook, rest one of the salmon fillets, skin side down, on a large sheet of baking paper. Spoon the filling on top of the fillet, pressing it down firmly all the way to the edges. Lay the second fillet, skin side up, over the filling to make a salmon 'sandwich'. Season the outside of the fish with salt and pepper. Bring up the sides of the baking paper to wrap and cover the fish completely. Then spread out the newspaper and lift the fish on to it, wrapping it up in a bundle. Use string to tie and secure the newspaper in several places – you might want to enlist a second pair of hands so you can get the knots good and tight.

Now lift the fish parcel and hold it under a gently running cold tap to dampen the newspaper all over. This stops it burning in the heat of the oven. Lay it on a large baking sheet and slide it into the oven to bake for 1–1¼ hours. Use a skewer to pierce through to the thickest part of the fish, holding it there for 30 seconds. Press the tip of the skewer to your bottom lip; it should feel nicely hot, not burning, if the salmon is cooked through. If it is on the cool side, cook for another 10 minutes and then check again.

Rest the parcel on a serving platter, then cut through the top of the newspaper and peel back the layers to reveal the fish below. Cut into chunky slices and serve with lemon wedges to squeeze over.

SALTED CARAWAY AND RYE CRACKERS

These crisp savoury crackers were designed to be eaten with the rillettes on page 183, but they go well with any other charcuterie, pâté or cheese as well. If you want to serve them with the rillettes, make them before you slide the pork in, when the oven is hotter. The temperature here is not too critical – you are looking to dry out the crackers and give them a little colour, and it will just take less time or more depending on the heat you have to offer. They will keep for over a week in an airtight tin.

180–210°C (350–410°F)
MAKES ABOUT 28–30

125g (1 cup) plain (all-purpose) flour, plus a little for rolling
125g (1 cup) rye flour
1 tsp dark brown sugar
½ tsp baking powder
½ tsp fine salt
50g (¼ cup) butter, diced into cubes
125ml (½ cup) milk
1 egg, beaten
1–2 tbsp caraway seeds, to taste
sea salt flakes

Put both flours, the sugar, baking powder and salt into a mixing bowl and stir together. Add the cubes of butter and rub between fingers and thumbs until it is incorporated into the flour, just like making crumble. Add the milk and bring together with a tablespoon to form a smooth dough. Wrap in clingfilm and allow to rest for 30 minutes at room temperature. You can make this a couple of hours in advance of baking if you want to get ahead.

When you are ready to bake, lightly flour the worktop and lightly flour a baking tray.

Roll out the dough so that it is approximately the shape of your baking tray and about 2mm (⅛in) thick, lifting and rotating it a little to make sure it's not sticking. You can trim the edges to make neat crackers if you like, but I generally prefer to leave them homemade and rustic-looking.

Roll the dough lightly around the rolling pin and lift it on to the tray, gently unrolling it. Prick all over with a fork, then deeply score into crackers – I rather like mine in diamond shapes, but any easily snappable shape is fine.

Crack the egg into a bowl and lightly whisk with a tablespoon of water. Brush all over the dough, then sprinkle over the caraway seeds and plenty of sea salt flakes.

Slide into the oven to bake (the door can be on or off), rotating halfway through cooking. Cook for about 15–20 minutes – they are done when they are deep golden brown and practically crisp all through; they will crisp up more on cooling. Once cool, snap the crackers along the score lines and store in an airtight tin.

AND ANOTHER THING...

● Substitute the caraway seeds with another spice like fennel, nigella or cumin.
● Or use other seeds like pumpkin, sunflower or sesame instead.

SALT-BAKED BEETROOT MAYONNAISE

Homemade mayo is a real treat for dunking seasonal veg in, but if you add salt-baked beetroot to the mix it's even better. An awesomely vivid colour with an earthy flavour, beetroot mayonnaise is spectacular in both looks and taste. Not limited to purple sprouting broccoli, this is good with other vegetables like asparagus or boiled new potatoes, or even grilled prawns, chicken or steak.

180°C (350°F)
MAKES A BOWLFUL, SERVING 6-ISH AS A STARTER OR PART OF A TAPAS-STYLE MEAL

2 eggs
750g (about 3 cups) fine table salt
2 medium/large beetroots (beets),
   raw, unpeeled (about 200g/
   7oz each)
1 tsp Dijon mustard
1 clove of garlic, roughly chopped
200ml (¾ cup) groundnut oil (or
   other flavourless oil)
50ml (¼ cup) extra virgin olive oil
1–2 tbsp white wine vinegar, to taste
salt and freshly ground black
   pepper

To serve
400–500g (14oz–1lb 2oz) purple
   sprouting broccoli
2 tbsp olive oil

Separate the eggs, putting the whites into a mixing bowl and the yolks into a small bowl. Refrigerate the yolks for making the mayonnaise later.

Add the salt to the egg white and mix well until it looks like damp sand. Take spoonfuls of the wet salt and pack it around each beetroot, using your hands to pat and stick it on. Cover each beetroot all over – the salt will form a good 1cm (½in) layer, totally enclosing each one. Set in a small roasting tin and slide into the oven to bake for 2 hours.

Meanwhile, blanch the broccoli in boiling water for a couple for minutes. Drain, and refresh under cold running water to stop it overcooking. Drain well again and tip on to a roasting tray. Drizzle over the olive oil and season with a little salt and pepper. Set aside.

Remove the beetroot from the oven, shutting the door to keep the heat in. The salt crust will be golden brown and baked solid by now. Using a tea towel to protect your hands, grasp one beetroot and with a firm twist pull it from the tin, leaving behind a baked base of salt. Use a table knife to ease away the rest of the salt case and repeat with the other beetroot. Peel the beets, reserve half of one for the garnish, and roughly chop the rest. Place in a food processor and purée to a really smooth paste. Spread out on a plate to cool quickly, then chill in the fridge while you make the mayonnaise.

Wash and dry the food processor bowl. Add the reserved egg yolks, mustard and garlic and whizz until thoroughly combined. Measure both oils into a jug and, with the motor running, add a few drops via the feeder tube. Allow the mixture to whizz for a few seconds, then add a few more drops. Once you the egg starts to thicken, you can add the oil a little faster, never more than a very thin trickle, all the while leaving the motor running. Don't rush adding the oil or you risk splitting the mix.

Once all the oil is in, it's time to turn your mayo bright pink. Again with the motor running, add spoonfuls of the beetroot purée down the feeder tube. Once all the beetroot is in, add a tablespoon of vinegar and, once combined, stop the motor and taste. If it needs a little more vinegar, add another spoonful. Season with plenty of black pepper and perhaps a tiny bit of extra salt if you think it needs it. Spoon into a serving dish.

With any luck, your fire still has a good bit of heat left in it. Light another small fire in the centre using a natural fire lighter and a few thin 3-4cm logs, allowing it to burn steadily for 20 minutes or so until you have a good roasting flame. Slide the broccoli into the oven to roast for about 15 minutes until lightly charred in a few places. To serve, arrange the broccoli on a plate and serve alongside the bowl of beetroot mayo for dipping.

4

COOLING

**USING THE DYING EMBERS
AND FALLING TEMPERATURES**

USING THE DYING EMBERS
AND FALLING TEMPERATURES

Once you have finished pizza-making, roasting, grilling and baking, there will still be a large sink of heat energy within your oven's walls and floor. If your oven is well-insulated around the sides, over the top and on the base too, you basically have yourself a giant slow cooker and here are loads of ideas for the very best of low and slow baking and roasting, braising and overnight cooking.

I have divided this chapter into two – those recipes that take up to 4 hours, and those that you can leave in your oven all night. With the recipes that suggest overnight cooking, I tend to fire up my oven during the afternoon, then cook on it throughout the evening, and these are the recipes I have planned and have ready to shove into the oven just before bed, to maximize the wonderful steady, slowly falling heat the oven provides overnight. Obviously if you are up with the larks and baking pizza for elevenses, then your oven cooling phase will come earlier in the day, so for 'overnight' read simply a cooling oven. Either way, 'overnight recipes' are those that take 7–10, or even more, hours.

To maximize the fuel efficiency of your oven, I would suggest you try to always have a dish or two prepped and ready for this kind of cooking. Sometimes that can be as simple as shoving in a pot of dried beans (see page 168), or it could be as satisfying as getting the next day's brunch or lunch ready, or even baking your Christmas cake (see page 185).

If you do not have an insulated oven, I'm sorry to say that many of the slower cooking recipes in this chapter might be a bit of struggle because your oven may lose heat too quickly. Every oven is different, and over time you will learn to gauge how your particular oven responds after firing, how soon it cools and how steep that curve of falling energy is. If you have yet to buy or build your oven, I would strongly recommend making sure it is thoroughly insulated all round, including under the floor, to maximize the range of cooking you can use it for.

COOLING AN OVEN THAT IS TOO HOT

Often, frustratingly, you will find yourself trying to get a cool oven hotter by adding more fuel, but just occasionally, if you have had a fantastic cooking session with a well-fired oven, you will find that it's rather hotter than it needs to be to cook many of the recipes here. So you need to cool it down, and while leaving the door off will work, I find sometimes it cools too slowly. A much better way is to slide in a big pan – like a stockpot – of cold water. The fire you have lit has created a certain amount of energy, and you need to lose that energy, much of which happens as it is transferred into your food. By adding cold water in a pan, which will come up to the boil really quite fast in a hot oven, you are transferring that energy away into the water. And the bonus is a pan of hot water to add to the washing-up in the sink!

EQUIPMENT FOR SLOW COOKING

For this chapter, really anything goes for cooking in – as long as it has no plastic or wooden handles it will be fine. Terracotta and earthenware dishes and casseroles are great, as is cast iron. Covering things with lids or foil helps prevent drying out over long cooking times, and in a few recipes (like the barbecoa beef on page 175, the beef rendang on page 176, and the lamb tangia on page 172) you'll see I suggest covering food with damp greaseproof paper to help keep the moisture in. While some recipes, like the beggar's chicken on page 159, come wrapped in their own protective casing.

Some recipes need a really gentle heat – like the Christmas cake on page 185 and the pavlova meringue base on page 166. For these I have suggested you raise them up above the floor or the fire by placing them on a cooling rack, or anything you might use as a grill in your oven (see page 46 for grilling). I have even used a spare ridged terracotta roof tile to rest things on, to lift them up if the floor of the oven is too hot.

SLOW ROAST LAMB SHOULDER WITH FENNEL AND GARLIC

A whole lamb shoulder makes a wonderful and generous celebratory roast, and the long slow cooking time is perfect for the wood-fired oven treatment. Here I cook it for a good 3 hours in total, but it's such a forgiving joint, you could easily leave it for 4 hours and it would be just fine, as long as your oven is not running too hot and it has a loose tent of foil to stop it over-browning. I like to serve this roast with either the unctuous dauphinoise potatoes on page 151 or their more humble cousin, boulangère potatoes (page 150), sliding them into the oven alongside the lamb about 1½ hours before I want to eat.

180–220°C (350–425°F)
SERVES ABOUT 6

2 tbsp fennel seeds
1 tbsp black peppercorns
6 fat cloves of garlic, roughly
   chopped
1 tbsp olive oil
1 tsp salt flakes
1 x 2.2–2.4kg (5lb–5lb 4oz) lamb
   shoulder, bone in
2 large onions, sliced
400–500g (14oz–1lb 2oz) carrots,
   small to medium, scrubbed
salt and freshly ground black
   pepper

Put the fennel seeds and peppercorns into a pestle and mortar and crush coarsely. Add the garlic, olive oil and salt and pound together to make a paste.

Rest the lamb in a large roasting tin and use a sharp knife to pierce lots of little slits all over. Spoon the fennel seed paste over the lamb and rub it all over, massaging it into the slits as much as possible. Cover and chill for a few hours, or overnight if you have time.

A couple of hours before you want to cook, remove the lamb from the fridge and let it come up to room temperature.

Slide it into the oven to roast for an hour. After an hour, loosely cover the tin with foil and put back into the oven for another hour. Then scatter the onions and whole carrots around the lamb, turning them to baste in the juices, and return to the oven for a final hour, after which time everything should be really tender.

Lift the lamb on to a serving platter and arrange the vegetables alongside, spooning over any juices from the pan.

GREEK BUTTER BEAN AND TOMATO SOUP WITH OREGANO, FETA AND OLIVES

This hearty, healthy bean soup is packed full of sunshine flavours and is really easy to make. Butter beans are one of the pulses that I find quite hard to cook by boiling, as the inside can go mushy before the outside is tender, leading to a big collapsed mess when you drain them, but if you bake them in the wood oven they cook beautifully, as they never boil vigorously. The bicarbonate of soda may seem like a slightly odd addition but it just helps to soften the butter bean skins which can be a little tough. You could, in theory, leave this soup to cook overnight and certainly it would taste fine, but with really long slow cooking you might lose some of the summery vibrancy from the tomatoes.

ABOUT 180–210°C (350–410°F)
SERVES 6–8

2 tbsp olive oil
2 onions, chopped
3 stalks of celery, finely chopped
3 cloves of garlic, crushed
2 bay leaves
1 tsp dried oregano
½ tsp ground cinnamon
750g (1lb 10oz) tomatoes, chopped
2 tbsp tomato purée
300g (1½ cups) dried butter beans
½ tsp bicarbonate of soda
    (baking soda)
salt and freshly ground black
    pepper

For the garnish
200g (1 cup) feta cheese, crumbled
a handful of pitted Kalamata olives,
    chopped
zest of 1 lemon
1 clove of garlic, finely chopped
a small bunch of fresh oregano,
    leaves picked and chopped

Put the oil, onions and celery into a large heavy-based pan – a cast-iron casserole is ideal. Slide into the oven to soften for 10–15 minutes. Add the garlic, bay leaves, oregano and cinnamon, stir well to mix, and slide back into the oven for a further 5 minutes. Stir in the tomatoes and tomato purée and add 1½ litres (6 cups) of cold water. Season with salt and freshly ground black pepper, tip in the butter beans and sprinkle in the bicarbonate of soda (baking soda). Give everything a good stir, cover with a lid, or a snug-fitting piece of foil, and slide into the oven to slowly braise for 2½–3 hours, after which time the beans should be tender.

At this point you can cool, chill and freeze your soup until you are ready to eat it, or you can eat it straight away. Either way, when you are ready to serve, make sure your soup is piping hot.

Make the garnish by stirring together the feta, olives, lemon zest, garlic and oregano. Ladle the soup into bowls and sprinkle a little of the garnish on top.

GAMMON, BAKED POTATOES AND THYME-ROAST LEEKS

Thick slices of juicy gammon and fluffy baked potatoes anointed with oodles of butter – this is a simple and delicious old-school dinner and just the sort of thing that would be very welcome after a hard day's baking, especially on a slightly chilly day. My kids would insist on a mound of grated cheese in their spuds – in their minds one never goes without the other – but I'm pretty content with just the boozy, buttery leeks alongside.

180-200°C (350-400°F)
SERVES 4

1 x 1–1.2kg (2¼–2½lb) piece of
  gammon, smoked or unsmoked
2 tbsp olive oil
4 medium baking potatoes
25g (2 tbsp) butter
3 large leeks, washed, trimmed
  and sliced into 3cm (1¼in)
  diagonal rings
150ml (¾ cup) white wine
4–5 sprigs of fresh thyme
freshly ground black pepper

To serve
plenty of butter, maybe
  some grated cheese

The oven temperature is not critical for this recipe – it's one of those brilliantly forgiving dishes that will take more or less time depending on the heat you have available. Ideally you want the oven running around 190–200°C (375–400°F), and you can expect it to take a couple of hours, during which time you have to do very little.

Place the gammon in a medium roasting tin – it needs to be big enough to hold the leeks too – and drizzle over the olive oil. Season with a little black pepper, but there's no need for any salt. Slide the tin into the oven, covering loosely with foil if your oven is running a little on the hot side. Shut the door, or leave it a little ajar if there are any live flames.

Score a few lines across the potatoes and sit them snugly in a small roasting tin, sliding it into the oven alongside the gammon. If you can't fit two trays in your oven, simply wrap each potato in foil and tuck them around the edges of the oven, wherever they'll fit, but ideally away from any embers.

After an hour, check the gammon, removing the foil if it has been covered. Add the butter to the roasting tin and let it melt. Then add the leeks, white wine, thyme and a good grind of pepper. Stir about a bit, then slide the tin back into the oven. At the same time, check the potatoes, moving them around a bit if any feel as if they are cooking quicker than the others. Cook for another 50–60 minutes, stirring the leeks once or twice during that time. If you want to double-check that the gammon is cooked, it should read about 70°C (158°F) on a meat thermometer.

Allow the gammon to rest for a few minutes, then carve into thick slices and serve on warm plates, with the baked potatoes cut and topped with butter, and the leeks spooned alongside.

TWO MELTING POTATO DISHES

Both these dishes are happy in a fairly wide range of heat (about 180–220°C/350–425°F), once again taking more or less time depending on what the oven has to offer. You may need to cover them with foil if they are colouring too quickly. The cream-based dauphinoise will have more of a tendency to burn than the stock-based boulangère.

BOULANGÈRE POTATOES

Boulangère potatoes (meaning 'baker's wife's potatoes' in French) are the original baker's trick for using the dying heat of the wood-fired oven to make a meal with heat that would otherwise be wasted. And what a wise trick it is: potatoes cooked until meltingly tender yet crispy on top, a great thing to serve alongside roast fish or chicken (try it with the flat roast chicken on page 76).

180–200°C (350–400F)
SERVES 4–6

1–1.2kg (2¼–2½lb) floury potatoes
2 large onions, thinly sliced
2 cloves of garlic, sliced
a handful of fresh sage leaves, finely chopped
500ml (2 cups) vegetable or chicken stock
50g (¼ cup) butter, cut into small cubes
salt and freshly ground black pepper

Peel the potatoes and slice them thinly into 3–4mm (1¼–1½in) rounds, using a mandoline if you have one. Spread about a third of the potatoes into a deep baking dish and top with about half the onions, garlic and sage. Season well with salt and pepper. Add another third of the potatoes, followed by the rest of the onion, garlic and sage. Finish with a final layer of potatoes, then gently pour in the stock. Dot the top with the butter and finish with a little more salt and pepper.

Slide the dish into the hot oven and cook until the top is crisp and the potatoes are really tender. This will take about 1¼–1½ hours, depending on the oven heat. Cover with foil if necessary to stop it colouring too much.

DAUPHINOISE POTATOES

Dauphinoise potatoes are essentially a supremely decadent version of boulangère potatoes, opposite, and they are my number-one desert-island potato dish. It had better be a rather chilly desert island, for this is surely not a recipe for the tropics but a rib-sticking, heavenly marriage of cream, garlic and potatoes. Perfect comfort food for a cold day. (See picture on page 145.)

180–200°C (350–400F)
SERVES 4–6

1–1.2kg (2¼–2½lb) floury potatoes
2 cloves of garlic, finely chopped
500ml (2 cups) double (heavy)
    cream
salt and freshly ground black
    pepper

Peel the potatoes and slice them thinly into 3–4mm (1¼–1½in) rounds, using a mandoline if you have one. Layer about a third of the potatoes in a baking dish and sprinkle over half the garlic. Season with a little salt and pepper, then add another third of the potatoes. Scatter over the remaining garlic, season once more and follow with the rest of the potatoes. Gently pour over the cream, allowing it to puddle through the slices. Finish with a final grind of salt and pepper.

Slide the dish into the hot oven and cook until the top is golden and the potatoes are soft and tender. This will take about 1¼–1½ hours, depending on the heat you give them. Loosely cover the top of the dish with foil if it is colouring too much.

BAKED APPLES WITH SPICED RUM RAISINS

Baked apples are a brilliantly forgiving thing to shove into the oven once you've finished cooking everything else you want to cook. They are happy to bake at pretty much whatever temperature you offer them, simply taking a little longer or a little less time depending on the heat available. I have given this recipe for a single apple wrapped in its own little foil parcel, as I would definitely make this just for myself if the oven was on anyway. Simply scale up to suit how many apples you want to cook, wrapping each separately and lining them up on a baking sheet.

I usually use smallish Bramley apples for this, as I love the mouth explosion you get from intensely sharp apple mixed with a really sweet spicy filling, which just gets even better when served with a big dollop of creamy vanilla ice cream. If you want slightly less of a rollercoaster going on in your mouth, try a firm dessert apple like a Braeburn.

ABOUT 180°C (350°F)
SERVES 1, BUT EASILY SCALED UP

2 tbsp raisins
1 tbsp dark brown sugar
a good pinch of mixed spice
1 tbsp golden rum (I like Havana
   Club)

To serve
a little cube of butter
vanilla ice cream or thick double
   (heavy) cream

In a small bowl, mix the raisins, sugar, spice and rum together and set aside for an hour or so, to let the fruit soak up the rum a little. If you have a microwave, give the mix a 30-second blast to help get things moving in the right direction.

Meanwhile, use an apple corer or a small sharp knife to cut the core from the centre of the apple, then score a fine line round the equator to help prevent it bursting as it bakes.

Tear off a square of tin foil and set the apple in the middle, drawing the sides of the foil up around it. Spoon the filling into the hole, pressing down firmly, and pour in any leftover rum. Top with a little cube of butter, then seal the foil tightly on top, drawing it up like a little purse. Repeat with the rest of your apples if you are making more than one, and set aside until you are ready to cook. You can stuff and wrap the apples a good few hours before you bake them.

Set on a roasting sheet or metal plate and slide it into the oven to bake. At around 180°C (350°F) the apple will take about 35–40 minutes, but it will happily cook in a cooler oven for longer, or cook even more quickly in a slightly hotter oven. The apple is ready when it yields with a giving squish if you squeeze the foil parcel.

AND ANOTHER THING...

● Replace the rum with brandy, or use orange or cranberry juice for a booze-free version.
● Swap the raisins for chopped dried apricots, dates or figs.
● If you have any leftover Christmas mincemeat hanging around, use that to stuff the apples instead of the fruit mix above.

BLACK BADGER PEA SALAD WITH AVOCADO AND PRAWNS

A British chickpea of sorts, black badger peas are a relatively new ingredient to me but they are really worth seeking out. With a deep, dark colour and lovely nutty flavour, these peas work brilliantly in this colourful Mexican-inspired salad. Like chickpeas, black badgers cook perfectly from dried in the gentle steady heat of the wood-fired oven. This recipe also uses a higher heat to roast red peppers and chillies, to give them a lovely mellow flavour, and also to make crunchy tortillas, both of which you can do well ahead of time when your oven is good and hot. All in all, this recipe is a very good use of your oven's range of temperatures.

180°C (350°F)
SERVES 4-6

To roast
2 red peppers
2 red chillies
4 flour tortillas
1 tbsp olive oil
½ tsp smoked paprika

To simmer
400g (2 cups) dried black badger
   peas
1 onion, halved through the root
   and peeled
2 whole cloves of garlic, bruised
2 bay leaves
1 tsp bicarbonate of soda
   (baking soda)

For the salad
3 fat limes
2 tbsp runny honey
75ml (⅓ cup) olive oil
200g (7oz) cherry tomatoes,
   quartered
½ a bunch of spring onions
   (scallions), finely sliced
50g (1 cup) fresh coriander
   (cilantro), roughly chopped
   (½ a large bunch)
2 large ripe avocados, peeled and
   diced
200g (7oz) cooked cold-water prawns
salt and freshly ground black
   pepper

Ideally, begin this salad when the oven has a good bit of heat in it, about 230-240°C (450-460°F), to roast some of the components, then the black badger peas get a long simmer once the oven has cooled to about 180°C (350°F).

When the oven is still hot, lay the whole red peppers and chillies in a small roasting tin and slide into the oven to roast for about 20 minutes, until they are soft and lightly charred. Tip into a bowl, cover with clingfilm and set aside for the skin to loosen as they cool.

Lay the tortillas in a stack and use a sharp knife to cut them through into about 12 wedges, like cutting a cake. Spread out on a couple of baking sheets and brush with the oil. Sprinkle over the smoked paprika and slide into the oven to crisp up for around 10–15 minutes. Allow to cool on the baking sheets and set aside until you are ready to assemble the salad.

Once the oven has cooled to 180°C (350°F) or thereabouts, put the black badger peas into a large saucepan or terracotta casserole and cover with double their volume of cold water. Add the onion halves, garlic cloves, bay leaves and bicarbonate of soda. Cover with a lid or a snugly tucked piece of foil, and slide into the oven for about 1½-2 hours, by which time the peas should be soft.

While the peas are cooking, make the dressing in a large mixing bowl. Finely grate the zest of 2 of the limes into the bowl, then squeeze in the juice of all 3. Drizzle in the honey and mix together with a whisk. Drizzle in the oil, whisking until the dressing has emulsified. Season to taste with salt and pepper.

Peel the skin from the peppers and chillies. Slice each in half and discard the seeds. Cut the peppers into strips and finely chop the chillies, then add both to the bowl of dressing, along with the tomatoes, spring onions and coriander.

Drain the peas, discarding the onion, garlic and bay leaves, and briefly run them under cold water to cool a little. Drain well, then tip into the mixing bowl while still just warm, stirring until combined. Lightly toss in the avocado and pile on to a serving platter. Scatter the prawns over the top and serve immediately, with the tortilla chips alongside.

GARLIC CHICKEN STEW WITH BLACK OLIVES AND BASIL DUMPLINGS

This chicken stew is packed full of Mediterranean flavours, thanks to a heady combination of wine, olives, orange and basil. The hearty dumplings mean that all you really need to serve alongside is something crisp and green – some buttery, dark green cabbage or kale, or maybe a big bowl of green salad, would be perfect.

180°C (350°F)
SERVES 4

For the stew
1–1.2kg (2lb 4oz–2lb 10oz) chicken thighs, skin on, bone in
1 tbsp plain (all-purpose) flour
1 tbsp olive oil
a good handful of Kalamata olives (about 75–100g/½ cup)
6 fat cloves of garlic, bruised and peeled
3 wide strips of orange zest, pared with a vegetable peeler
200ml (¾ cup) white wine
200ml (¾ cup) chicken stock

For the dumplings
200g (1½ cups) self-raising flour, plus extra for dusting
100g (1 cup) vegetable or beef suet
a large bunch of fresh basil
salt and freshly ground black pepper

AND ANOTHER THING...

• Use flat-leaf parsley in the dumplings, and use chopped parsnips and carrots instead of olives for a more traditional stew.
• Lose the orange peel and replace it with some woody herbs – thyme, rosemary or a couple of bay leaves.
• Swap the olives for a tablespoon or two or capers if you prefer.

Lay out the chicken on a plate and sprinkle over the flour. Season with a little salt and pepper and toss the chicken about a bit so it's evenly coated.

Put the oil into a wide, heavy-bottomed casserole dish – ideally you want the chicken to fit in it in a single layer (cast iron or sturdy terracotta is perfect) – and slide it into the oven for a couple of minutes to get hot. Remove it from the oven and add the chicken, skin side down, then slide back in for 30 minutes to allow the chicken to brown a little. Don't worry, it won't get really brown and crisp at this stage but by the time it's finished cooking it will be.

Remove the dish from the oven and turn the chicken skin side up. Scatter the olives and bruised garlic cloves around, and tuck in the orange peel. Pour in the wine and stock, and season well with salt and freshly ground black pepper. Slide back into the oven, shut the door and cook uncovered for 1 hour. The chicken will be starting to get lovely and crisp where the skin is above the liquid.

Meanwhile, make the dumplings. Stir together the flour and suet in a mixing bowl, seasoning well with salt and pepper. Finely chop two-thirds of the basil, reserving the rest for the garnish, using the leaves and the tender stalks as well. Add to the bowl and stir well to combine. Add just enough cold water to bring the dumplings together as a stiff but elastic dough, about 7–8 tablespoons. Tip on to a lightly floured worktop and knead briefly, then cut into 8 evenly sized pieces. Roll each piece into a ball and set aside on a lightly floured plate.

Once the chicken has had its hour, slide the dish out of the oven and arrange the dumplings on top. Slide back in and cook for another hour, after which time the dumplings should be crisp on top and cooked through, and the chicken so tender it's falling off the bone. Scatter over the rest of the basil, roughly chopped, just before serving.

BEGGAR'S CHICKEN

This intriguing Chinese recipe has a lot of historical, almost mythical, references to its provenance involving a beggar and an emperor. Originally the chicken would be stuffed, wrapped in lotus leaves, followed by a really thick layer of clay, before being buried in glowing embers to cook slowly. A recipe that sounded just perfect for cooking low and slow in the dying heat of a wood oven. Here the chicken is filled with a delicious shiitake mushroom stuffing, then wrapped in a more domestic-friendly salt dough before baking. You don't eat the dough, it just forms a sturdy case to hold the chicken, so don't worry too much about investing in top-quality salt – standard table salt is fine.

180°C (350°F)
SERVES 4–6

1 x 1.7-1.8kg (3lb 12oz–4lb) fresh chicken
1 egg
finely sliced spring onions (scallions) and chopped red chillies, to garnish
steamed rice, to serve

For the salt dough
1.5kg (about 11 cups) plain (all-purpose) flour, plus a little for rolling
300g (1¼ cups) fine salt

For the stuffing
15g (about ½ cup) dried shiitake mushrooms
125g (2 cups) fresh shiitake or chestnut mushrooms, finely chopped
5 spring onions (scallions), finely chopped
3 cloves of garlic, crushed
a thumb-sized piece of fresh ginger, grated
3 tbsp soy sauce
freshly ground black pepper

Put the flour into a mixing bowl and stir in the salt. Pour in just enough cold water to bring it together as a stiff dough. Start with 600–700ml (2½–3 cups) and work upwards slowly. You don't want it to be too wet, it just needs to be rollable. Tip the dough on to the worktop and knead briefly until it's smooth. Let it rest for 30 minutes at room temperature.

Meanwhile, make the stuffing for the chicken. Put the dried shiitake into a small heatproof glass and pour in 5 tablespoons of boiling water. Set aside to soak for 10 minutes, then finely chop, reserving the soaking water. Put the fresh mushrooms, spring onions, garlic, ginger and soy sauce into a bowl and stir together. Tip in the dried mushrooms, along with their soaking water, season well with black pepper and stir well. You can chill the stuffing in the fridge for a few hours, or even overnight if you want to get ahead.

Fill the cavity of the chicken with the stuffing, then tuck the legs in, tying with string so they are secure. If they stick out they may pierce through the dough. Brush a little soy sauce all over the bird, and season well with a good grind of black pepper.

Lightly flour the worktop and roll out the dough to a good 1½cm (⅝in) thick oval – it should be about 40 x 48cm (16 x 19in). You need to be able to wrap it generously around the chicken without stretching or tearing it, so it needs to be nice and thick and of ample size.

Carefully lift this dough into a large baking dish, allowing the overhang (there will be lots of it!) to rest around the dish on the worktop. Take the stuffed chicken and rest it breast side up in the centre of the dough. Draw the sides of the dough up and over the top of the bird, treating it really gently and trying your best not to pierce it. If it does crack, press it back together as best you can. Crimp the dough all along the top, just like sealing up a giant pasty. Brush the dough all over with the beaten egg.

Slide the baking dish into the oven, shut the door and leave entirely alone for 3 hours, after which time the crust will be baked solid and a lovely shiny golden brown. If your crust was a little weak in places, some juices may have leaked out into the dish; not to worry, you can just spoon them over the chicken as you carve.

Present the whole bird, still wrapped in dough, to your guests for maximum visual effect, then take a sharp knife to cut away the top of the dough to reveal the succulent bird within. Sprinkle with the chilli and spring onion slices before carving. Spoon out the stuffing and serve alongside, along with spoonfuls of the cooking liquor. Discard the crust.

SLOW ROAST QUINCE WITH HONEY AND SPICE

Quinces are such a rare treat and pretty hard to come by unless you are lucky enough to know someone with a tree or you live near a particularly good greengrocer. You certainly won't find them in the supermarket. They look and feel like a cross between a really hard pear and a funny wonky-looking apple, and I just love the dense, almost fudgy, texture they take on when they are cooked. You certainly have to cook them – they are completely inedible raw, and a long slow roasting time makes them a perfect fruit for using up the heat in your oven. Once baked, store them in the fridge in their syrup and they will last for at least a week. I like to eat them with thick Greek yoghurt for breakfast, perhaps scattered with a few pistachios or walnuts. They are also delicious with vanilla ice cream for an easy pudding, or try them as the fruit layer in an unusual trifle, maybe with a splash of Marsala or sweet sherry glugged in for good measure.

180°C (350°F)
MAKES A BIG BOWLFUL, ENOUGH FOR ABOUT 6 BREAKFASTS OR 1 BIG TRIFLE

juice of 1 lemon
1kg (2lb 4oz) quinces (about 4–5 smallish ones)
6 green cardamom pods
1 vanilla pod
100g (about ⅓ cup) runny honey

Fill a large mixing bowl with cold water and squeeze in the lemon juice. Peel and core the quinces – taking care, as they can be pretty tough to cut. Cut into wedges – quarters if they are on the small size, or into 6 pieces if they are larger – dropping them into the lemon water as you go. This will slow down the browning, as they are prone to quick oxidization.

Once they are all peeled and chopped and you are ready to cook, drain away the water and tip the quinces into a roasting tin. You want them to fit in a fairly snug single layer.

Bruise the cardamom pods with the flat of a large knife so they are open, then tip into the tin. Split the vanilla pod open and scrape out the seeds, then add them to the tin, along with the pod. Drizzle over the honey and pour on 100ml (⅓ cup) of water. Stir to mix the spice about a bit, then cover with foil and slide into the oven to roast for about an hour. Remove the foil and cook uncovered for another 30–60 minutes, pulling out the tin and turning the quinces over a few times to baste them in the syrup. They are done when they are really tender, have turned a deep orangey red colour and the syrup has reduced.

Allow to cool in the tin, then transfer them to a bowl, pour the syrup over and chill until required.

AND ANOTHER THING...

• Try swapping the spices; cinnamon and star anise are both lovely.

SMOKED PRAWN BISQUE

This luxurious-tasting soup has rather humble provenance, as you make it with the shells and heads left over after you've peeled and eaten the delicious smoked prawns on page 56. If you've never made a prawn bisque before, you'll be utterly surprised at the amount of intense seafood flavour you can squeeze out of something you would normally just throw in the bin. Once you've made the base stock, you can cool and chill it overnight in the fridge before carrying on with the soup the following day. It freezes brilliantly too, so you can make the stock at the end of one glorious seafood meal and freeze it so you have the beginnings of another at some other time.

180°C (350°F)
SERVES 4–6

1 tbsp olive oil
1 large onion, finely chopped
1 carrot, finely chopped
3 tbsp brandy (optional)
prawn heads and shells from the
    smoked prawns (recipe on page
    56) (from 600g/1lb 5oz) prawns)
1 clove of garlic, chopped
a pinch of chilli flakes
1 bay leaf
3 large vine tomatoes, chopped
100ml (⅓ cup) double (heavy)
    cream, plus a little extra
    to garnish
a few snipped chives, to garnish
salt and freshly ground black
    pepper

Put the olive oil, onion and carrot into a large heavy-based saucepan and slide into the oven, allowing to soften for 10 minutes, stirring once or twice. If you are using brandy, pour it in and slide the pan back into the oven for another 5 minutes, or until it's pretty much evaporated.

Add the prawn heads and shells, garlic, chilli flakes and bay leaf, stir to mix, and return to the oven for 5 minutes. Stir in the tomatoes, along with 800ml (3¼ cups) of cold water. Season with a little salt and pepper, cover with a lid and slide back into the oven for 1 hour.

At this point you can simply allow the stock to cool and chill overnight in the fridge, assuming it may now be the end of the evening, or you can carry on and finish the soup. Allowing the stock, shells and all, to cool in the pan will give you maximum flavour, and this is usually what I do.

When you are ready to carry on with the soup, use a stick blender to purée it until the shells are finely ground. Pour through a fine sieve into a clean pan, pushing with the back of a wooden spoon to extract maximum flavour from the prawn debris. If you are planning to freeze your soup base for another time, this is the moment to do it. Alternatively, set the pan over a medium heat and bring up to a simmer. Pour in the cream, stir to mix, and check the seasoning, adding a little more if necessary.

Pour into warmed bowls, and garnish with a little extra swirl of cream and a sprinkle of chives. Serve immediately.

ONE-PAN BAKED CHICKEN AND TOMATO BIRYANI

Laying no claims to authenticity at all, this one-pan, biryani-inspired bake is a great slow-cooking dish to shove into the oven at the end of a day's baking. It will putter away happily for a few hours while you have a well-earned rest. The spices are entirely optional – this is another dish that you should feel free to tweak and twiddle as you please (see below for a couple of ideas).

160–170°C (325–335°F)
SERVES 4

For the biryani spice blend
1 tbsp coriander seeds
1 tbsp cumin seeds
1–2 tsp chilli flakes, to taste
5 cardamom pods
2 bay leaves, fresh or dried, finely
   chopped
½ tsp ground mace
½ tsp ground cinnamon

For the biryani
300g (1½ cups) wholegrain
   brown rice
1 x 400g (14oz) tin of chopped
   tomatoes
2 onions, finely chopped
3 cloves of garlic, finely chopped
750ml (3¼ cups) chicken stock
8 chicken thighs (skin on, bone in)
50g (¼ cup) butter, diced
a handful of fresh coriander
   (cilantro), roughly chopped,
   to serve
salt and freshly ground black
   pepper

You need the oven to be running at about 160–170°C/325–335°F.

For the spice blend, put the coriander, cumin, chilli flakes and cardamom pods into a small frying pan and set over a medium heat to toast. As soon as you can smell their aroma wafting up from the pan, tip them into a spice mill or a pestle and mortar. Add the bay leaves, mace and cinnamon and grind to a coarse powder. Set aside for a minute.

Put the rice, tomatoes, onions and garlic into a large baking dish or roasting tin. Pour in the stock and add half the spice powder and a grind of salt and pepper, stirring well to mix.

Rub the rest of the spice powder all over the chicken thighs and sit them on top of the rice, spaced out evenly. Push them a little underneath the liquid, leaving the skin raised above so its crisps up. Dot the butter over the top of the rice.

Loosely cover the top with foil, then slide the dish into the oven and bake for 2½–3 hours. Towards the end of baking you may want to remove the foil, to let the skin crisp up even more.

Scatter over a little fresh coriander before serving.

AND ANOTHER THING...

• **Mediterranean chicken rice** – use 1 teaspoon dried oregano, orange zest and black olives instead of spices. Scatter with chopped basil.
• **Caribbean chicken rice** – swap the spices for 2 teaspoons ground allspice, 1 teaspoon dried thyme, a thumb-size piece of grated fresh ginger and a chopped Scotch bonnet chilli. Serve with lime wedges to squeeze over.

BEST EVER PAVLOVA BASE, AND 4 WAYS TO DRESS IT

Meringues, either individual or one big one for a pavlova, are a fantastic way to smugly get every last drop of heat from your oven. You do need a really cool oven for this to work, so I tend to make meringues first thing in the morning after a big cooking session the previous day.

A little tip for egg white separation – you cannot get even a molecule of egg yolk in your whites when you make meringues, as they will refuse to foam up. I separate my eggs into individual glasses, so if I do mess up and break one yolk I don't ruin the whole batch.

100–110°C (210–225°F)
MAKES ONE LARGE PAVLOVA BASE, SERVING ABOUT 6

200g (1 cup) caster (superfine)
    sugar
3 large egg whites
1 tbsp cornflour (cornstarch)
1 tsp white wine vinegar
1 tsp vanilla extract

You also need a baking sheet
lined with baking paper.

Weigh the sugar in a heatproof bowl – metal or ceramic – and slide it into the warm oven (100–110°C/210–225°F). Leave it to heat through for 15 minutes.

Once the sugar is hot, put the egg whites into the bowl of a food mixer fitted with a whisk attachment. Whisk to stiff peaks, then add a third of the sugar and whisk for another minute or so. Add the remaining sugar, a third at a time, whisking well after each addition. Finally, add the cornflour, vinegar and vanilla and give the meringue a final good whisk.

Spoon the meringue on to the prepared baking sheet, levelling it out with the back of a spoon so it's about the size of a dinner plate. Make the edge 1cm or so higher than the middle, and swirl to create a few artful peaks.

Set the tray on a cooling rack to raise it up so it doesn't sit directly on the oven base, then slide it into the cool oven and shut the door tight. Leave to gently bake for about 3 hours, checking every hour. The meringue is ready when you can very gently lift it from the surface of the paper, although it will still be delicate and crack if you are heavy-handed. Allow to cool completely before topping. See below for a few ideas.

For each topping, start with a layer of whipped cream – simply whisk 300ml (1¼ cups) of double cream to soft billowy peaks and spoon and swirl it across the cooked meringue base. Then simply top with your favourite fresh fruit, or try one these ideas:

• **Nutty rum banoffee** – scatter 2 or 3 sliced ripe bananas over the cream. Beat 4 tablespoons of caramel sauce with a couple of teaspoons of rum (or boiling water if you prefer) in a small bowl until you can drizzle it (try a jar of dulce de leche, or caramelized condensed milk). Drizzle the sauce over the bananas and scatter over a handful of toasted chopped pecans.

• **Rhubarb and custard** – top with a pile of roasted or poached rhubarb (see page 122) and a generous drizzle of fresh vanilla custard. Scatter over a few toasted almonds too, if you like.

• **Lemon curd and raspberries** – add a few generous spoons of lemon curd in little dollops over the top of the cream, swirling it in with the spoon. Scatter on a couple of generous handfuls of raspberries. Again, a scatter of toasted nuts adds a lovely crunch – hazelnuts, pecans, almonds are all great.

• **Marsala cream, figs and chocolate** – add a couple of tablespoons of Marsala to the cream just before you whip it, then top with slices of ripe fig. Use a potato peeler to generously shave dark chocolate all over the top.

BEANS IN THE OVEN

Cooking dried beans doesn't need to be complicated, and they are a perfect thing for using up all your oven's residual heat. At its most straightforward, at the end of a long evening, just cover a bagful of beans with plenty of cold water, chuck in a couple of sprigs of herbs and a garlic clove or two, cover the pot and slide it into the oven. By morning you will have a panful of tender beans that you can drain and use however you like. If I haven't made a plan for anything else to use the dying heat, then I almost always do this. Beans double in weight from dried to cooked, so if you want 800g (4 cups) of cooked beans, start with 400g (2 cups) of dried beans. The cooked beans can then be bagged up in tin-sized amounts and frozen, ready for instant bean-iness at another time.

On the whole, there is no need to pre-soak your beans. The only exception is kidney beans, which need 8 hours soaking, and then a 10-minute hard boil on the hob, to kill off the toxin they contain. Other beans from the same group, such as butter beans, cannellini and pinto, contain much smaller amounts of the same toxin, but starting them off at 180°C (350°F) will mean they easily reach boiling point before the oven cools down. If I'm cooking beans at a higher temperature for less time (see the Greek bean soup on page 146, for example) I generally add a little pinch of bicarbonate of soda, which helps to soften the skins, but with a long overnight cook you don't need to do this.

BOSTON BAKED BEANS

I have made many versions of this recipe, using soaked, unsoaked and pre-cooked beans, and I am very happy to report that the best flavour comes from beans that are unsoaked and dry. Just chuck it all in the pot, slide it into the oven and go to bed, smug in the knowledge that brunch is sorted. All you will need to do is make lots of buttered toast, and maybe fry a few eggs to go on top.

180°C (350°F)
SERVES ABOUT 4

300g (10½oz) fatty piece of smoked bacon (use bacon offcuts), cut into 2–3cm (¾–1¼in) chunks
200g (1 cup) dried cannellini beans
100g (3½oz) cherry tomatoes, halved
1 onion, finely chopped
1 clove of garlic, crushed
½ tsp ground allspice
1 bay leaf
400ml (1½ cups) boiling water
2 tbsp black treacle
25g (⅛ cup) dark brown sugar
1 heaped tsp English mustard
salt and freshly ground black pepper

Put the bacon, unsoaked dried beans and tomatoes into a terracotta or earthenware casserole dish. Stir in the onion, garlic and allspice and tuck in the bay leaf.

Measure the boiling water in a jug, and set the tablespoon for measuring the treacle into it for a few seconds to get hot. Once hot, shake off the excess water and use the hot spoon to dip into the treacle and measure it out into the hot water – it should slide off without stickiness. Stir in the sugar and mustard until dissolved and season with a little salt and pepper. Pour over the beans, then cover the pot with a tight-fitting lid or snugly wrapped piece of foil.

Slide into a cool oven at the end of an evening's cooking, with a starting temperature of a good 180°C (350°F) or thereabouts – and leave overnight. Check the beans in the morning – after a good 10–11 hours they should be glorious, and will happily sit in the oven keeping hot until brunch.

SMOKY SPLIT PEA AND BACON SOUP

Like all pulses, split peas are great for absorbing other flavours, making them the perfect foil for a few spices. Here I've kept it simple with smoked paprika and enhanced the smokiness with smoked bacon. People are often surprised that wood-fired oven food doesn't really taste smoky, unless you help it along with actual smoke, or smoked-flavour things. This soup freezes brilliantly – pack it into portion-size servings for taking to work.

150–180°C (300–350F)
SERVES ABOUT 6

2 tbsp olive oil
200g (7oz) smoked bacon lardons
2 onions, finely chopped
2 cloves of garlic, crushed
1 tsp smoked paprika
500g (2½ cups) split peas
   (yellow or green)
2 litres (3½ pints) stock (vegetable,
   chicken or ham) or water
freshly ground black pepper

To serve
a little chopped fresh flat-leaf
   parsley
a sprinkle of smoked paprika
extra virgin olive oil

You want the oven running at about 180°C (350°F) for sautéing the bacon and onions, then a lower temperature of about 150°C (300°F) for the overnight cooking of the soup. Alternatively you can cook the soup quicker at a higher temperature if you don't want to leave it overnight – at 180°C (350°F) it will take about 2½–3 hours.

Put the oil, lardons and onions into a large saucepan and slide into the oven. Cook for 15–20 minutes, stirring regularly to make sure it all cooks evenly. You want the onions to soften and caramelize a little. Remove the pan from the oven and stir in the garlic and paprika. Set the pan aside until you have finished all the other cooking you plan to do in the oven and it is cooling down for the night. You can, of course, cook the bacon and onions on the hob indoors if your oven is too full of other things.

Once you are ready to get the soup cooking, simply add the split peas, stock and a good grind of black pepper. Give it a little stir, cover with a lid or a snugly fitting piece of foil, and slide into the oven, shutting the door tightly. The soup will cook happily and gently for 12 or more hours. Because of the gentle nature of the cooking the peas will become really soft and tender but they won't necessarily break down to form a cohesive, thick soup. You can use a potato masher to break up the peas, stirring together if you prefer a more dhal-like texture; or blitz with a stick blender for a smooth soup.

Check the seasoning – you may want to add a little salt or extra pepper. Serve while piping hot, sprinkled with a little parsley and extra paprika, and a good drizzle of extra virgin olive oil.

AND ANOTHER THING...

• Lose the bacon and smoked paprika and add a few curry-like spices – a generous sprinkle of cumin seeds, a little ground cinnamon, a few cardamom pods, some freshly grated ginger, a pinch of chilli. Serve with a drizzle of natural yoghurt and a sprinkle of chopped fresh coriander (cilantro).

MOROCCAN SLOW-BAKED LAMB TANGIA

A tangia (not to be confused with a tagine, which is more stew-like) is a classic Moroccan dish from Marrakech. The tangia is the name of the vessel this slow-braised dish is cooked in – an earthenware vase really, with a fairly narrow neck, which I don't have, so I use an old earthenware casserole dish which works just fine. A deep rather than shallow shape is preferable, and keeping the whole thing sealed is key to stopping it drying out, hence the damp baking paper and foil approach. A genuine tangia would have no chickpeas in, but I prefer to balance out my meat consumption with a bit more veg.

150–160°C (300–325°F)
SERVES 2 – EASY TO DOUBLE OR TREBLE THE RECIPE FOR MORE

a good pinch of saffron threads

300g (10½oz) boned lamb leg, diced into 4cm (1½in) pieces

1 onion, very finely chopped

3 cloves of garlic, chopped

½ a preserved lemon, skin finely chopped

1 tbsp cumin seeds

1 tsp white peppercorns, freshly ground

1 tsp ground turmeric

½ tsp ground ginger

a good pinch of salt

2 tbsp olive oil

1 x 400g (14oz) tin of chickpeas (garbanzo beans), drained and rinsed

a little chopped fresh coriander (cilantro), to serve

You need a cooling oven at a temperature of around 150°C (300°F) for this recipe. If it is a little hotter than that, raise the baking dish off the oven floor by placing it on a cooling rack. This will protect it a little from overcooking.

Put the saffron threads into a heatproof measuring jug and pour in 200ml (¾ cup) of boiling water. Set aside to soak for a few minutes while you assemble the tangia.

Put the meat, onion, garlic and preserved lemon into an earthenware braising dish and sprinkle over the cumin seeds, peppercorns, turmeric, ginger and a little salt. Drizzle with the oil, then, using either clean hands or a metal spoon, stir together really well so the meat is evenly coated. Scatter over the chickpeas, then pour in the saffron and its soaking water.

Tear off a generous piece of baking paper and run it under the cold tap, scrunching it up and unfolding it again so you have a nice damp sheet. Lay it over the dish, pressing it firmly down to compact the spiced meat and chickpeas. Tuck the edges in well, then do the same with a sheet of tin foil to seal the food in so that minimal liquid escapes. Top with a lid, or a final sheet of foil snugly wrapped over the top. Set aside until you are ready to cook. At this point you could shove the whole pot into the fridge and forget about it for up to 24 hours, if you want to prepare it well ahead of your wood-fire cooking session.

Once you have finished cooking for the day and your oven has developed an even heat through the floor and dome, and has cooled to about 150°C (300°F), you can slide the dish in, shut the door and forget about it overnight.

When the tangia is cooked you can cool it for reheating later, or freeze it for up to 3 months. To serve, reheat until piping hot, then scatter over the coriander. A dish of buttery couscous would be the perfect accompaniment.

BARBECOA BEEF BRISKET

This Mexican spiced beef is a brilliant overnight braise, one that is practically impossible to get wrong, as, cooked low and slow, brisket is a cut of beef that just gets better with time. I like to serve this beef pulled and stuffed into tortilla wraps, with plenty of guacamole and esquites, the gorgeous charred sweetcorn salad on page 63. You could also serve it with a big bowl of rice and beans, or even mashed potatoes for a really hearty lunch on a chilly day. If you don't fancy the barbecoa spicing, I've suggested a couple of other ways to flavour your braise below.

150–160°C (300–325°F)
SERVES ABOUT 6, GENEROUSLY

1.8kg (4lb) beef brisket
3 tbsp cider vinegar
2 tbsp olive oil
1 tbsp cumin seeds
2 tsp ancho chilli flakes, or to taste
2 tsp chipotle chilli flakes, or to taste
6 cloves
1 tsp dried oregano
2 bay leaves, finely chopped
1 large onion, chopped
½ a bulb of garlic, cloves peeled and roughly chopped
500ml (2 cups) beef stock
salt and freshly ground black pepper
chopped red chilli and fresh coriander (cilantro), to garnish

You need a steady low oven temperature of around 150–160°C (300–325°F).

If the brisket is rolled and tied with string, unroll it and open it out so you have a flat piece. Lay it in a large deep roasting tin, slicing it into two pieces if necessary so it fits in a single layer.

In a small bowl mix together the vinegar, oil, cumin seeds, chilli flakes, cloves, oregano, bay leaves and a little salt and freshly ground black pepper. Pour this over the meat and rub in well all over. Scatter over the onion and garlic, and turn the meat a few times so they are evenly distributed on both sides of the beef. At this point you can either set the meat aside until you are ready to cook, covered and in the fridge, or you can cook it straight away. It has such a long slow cooking time that it doesn't really need marinating, but it may suit you to get it ready ahead of time.

Pour the stock over the prepared brisket. Take a generous sheet of baking parchment and scrunch it up under running water. Unfold, shaking off the excess water, and tuck the parchment around the beef, creating a steamy blanket to keep it moist. Cover the tray with a tight-fitting sheet of foil and slide it into the oven. Leave to gently braise overnight. Check it in the morning, 8–10 hours later. It should be tender, falling apart and ready to eat, but at this point it will keep gently cooking until you want it – another 4–6 hours should be fine. I have left it very successfully for up to 16 hours. Depending on the heat left in your oven and how tightly fitting the lid was, the liquid around the beef may need reducing in the morning. If so, remove the foil and baking paper and refold the foil so it just covers the beef but leaves the liquid exposed, to reduce down for the final few hours.

To serve, lift the meat on to a platter, scatter with chilli and coriander, and tease apart with two forks. Pour the sauce into a jug or bowl to serve alongside.

AND ANOTHER THING...

• Red wine and balsamic vinegar – lose the spices, but keep the onion and garlic; swap half the stock for 250ml (1 cup) of red wine and add 5 tablespoons of balsamic vinegar and a few sprigs of fresh rosemary.
• Soy and ginger – swap the spices for 4 whole star anise and a teaspoon of Chinese five-spice powder. Add a generous thumb-sized piece of fresh ginger, finely chopped, and sub out 100ml (⅓ cup) of the stock for the same amount of dark soy sauce. Add a little chilli, fresh or dried, if you like. Garnish with sliced spring onions (scallions) and serve with plenty of rice.

INDONESIAN BEEF RENDANG

Rendang is a classic curry from Indonesia that is packed full of intense spices but not particularly hot, although you can always add more chilli if you want. This curry is a breeze to prepare, so it's a good candidate for using up the heat of your oven and getting a meal ready for later in the week, or even for shoving in the freezer for another day. Galangal is a very similar-looking root to ginger but the taste is rather different, a bit citrussy, with slightly pine-like aromas, and it's worth seeking out if you can – it's pretty easy to find in oriental grocers. On another note, I always cook with echalion shallots because they are so much easier to peel than those fiddly little fellas.

150–160°C (300–325°F)
SERVES 4–6

900g–1kg (2–2lb 4oz) beef shin, cut
    into 3–4cm (1¼–1½in) chunks
350g (12oz) shallots, ideally
    echalion (banana) shallots,
    roughly chopped
50g (about ⅓ cup) fresh ginger,
    roughly chopped
30g (1oz) galangal, roughly
    chopped
6 cloves of garlic, roughly chopped
1 tbsp ground turmeric
1 tbsp ground coriander seeds
    (ideally freshly ground)
2 tsp chilli flakes
1 tsp ground cinnamon
½ tsp ground cloves
1 x 400ml (14fl oz) tin of coconut
    milk
3 tbsp keçap manis (sweet soy
    sauce), or 2 tbsp dark soy sauce
    plus 1 tbsp soft brown sugar
1 tbsp tamarind concentrate
4–6 fresh or frozen lime leaves
salt and freshly ground black
    pepper

To garnish
halves of boiled egg
crispy fried onions
chopped fresh coriander (cilantro)
sliced bird's-eye chillies

You need a steady low oven temperature of around 150–160°C (300–325°F).

Put the beef into a cast-iron or earthenware casserole dish and season with a little salt and pepper. Set aside while you prepare the curry sauce.

Put the shallots, ginger, galangal and garlic into a food processor and pulse to a fairly smooth paste. Add the dried spices – the turmeric, coriander, chilli flakes, cinnamon and cloves – and pulse once more. Pour in the coconut milk, along with the keçap manis and tamarind, and pulse one last time until combined. Pour over the beef, giving it a little stir so the meat is coated in sauce. Finally, tuck in the lime leaves, spacing them out fairly evenly and pressing them under the sauce.

Tear off a sheet of greaseproof paper and scrunch it up under cold running water. Shake off the excess, unfold and tuck snugly over the beef, pressing it down on to the surface. Cover with a tight-fitting lid and set aside until you are ready to cook. You can get the dish completely ready several hours and even the day before, and leave it in the fridge ready to slide into the oven at the end of the day.

The rendang will cook very happily for 8–10 hours providing your oven isn't too hot. If your oven is on the hot side, set the casserole on a metal cooling rack in the oven to lift it away from the base.

To serve, spoon the rendang over rice (I like to serve it with yellow rice – simply add a good pinch of turmeric to the rice as it cooks) and scatter on the garnishes of your choice.

AND ANOTHER THING...

Beef shin is made for slow cooking, and it's very easy to switch the flavours around. Just keep the levels of liquid about the same, and the base of shallots (or indeed, onion) and garlic generous. Here are a couple of ideas:

● A traditional beef and ale stew – swap the coconut milk for a dark ale, lose all the spices and add woody herbs (bay leaf, rosemary) in their place. Add a chopped carrot and a parsnip with the shallots – no need to purée the onion and garlic, just chop them up and chuck them in. Great served with proper buttery mashed potato.

● A creamy green peppercorn stew – replace the coconut milk with 250ml (1 cup) of beef stock and 150ml (⅔ cup) of double cream. Chop the shallots and garlic rather than puréeing them, and add a chopped green pepper. Lose the spices and add 2 tablespoons of green peppercorns, drained from their brine. Great served with plain rice.

TWO OVERNIGHT NO-FUSS DIPS

No matter how tired you are, you can still utilize the dying temperatures to start off another meal. Here are two dips that involve shoving something in overnight with barely any thought whatsoever.

A ROASTED SQUASH DIP WITH MIDDLE EASTERN FLAVOURS

Inspired by the flavours of dukkah – a gorgeous Middle Eastern spice mix with thyme and hazelnuts – butternut squash becomes seriously sweet when roasted whole overnight.

ABOUT 140–150°C (275–300°F)
SERVES 4–6

1 large butternut squash
1 tsp each of chilli flakes, cumin seeds and coriander seeds
6 shelled hazelnuts
1 clove of garlic, roughly chopped
1 tbsp pomegranate molasses
1 tbsp olive oil
sea salt flakes
2 tbsp Greek yoghurt
a good squeeze of lemon juice, about 1 tbsp
a sprig of fresh thyme, leaves picked

Prick the squash all over a few times with the tip of a sharp knife. Rest it on a small baking tray and slide it into the centre of the oven. The next morning, remove the squash – it will be really soft all the way through and the skin will be bronzed and caramelized. Slice it in half, then scoop out and discard the seeds and membranes. Scoop the flesh away from the skin and put it into a food processor, blitzing to a really smooth purée. Add the garlic, pomegranate molasses and olive oil, and blitz again.

Tip the spices and the hazelnuts into a small frying pan and toast over a medium heat on the hob until fragrant. Remove the hazelnuts, roughly chop and set aside. Tip the spices into a pestle and mortar and add the salt flakes to help you grind to a coarse powder. Add the spice to the food processor and whizz again. Taste to check the seasoning and set aside to cool.

Meanwhile, in a small bowl, stir together the yoghurt, thyme and lemon juice, seasoning with a little salt and black pepper. Set aside.

Once the squash purée is cool, stir before serving, drizzle over the yoghurt mix and sprinkle over the chopped hazelnuts. Serve at room temperature.

OVERNIGHT HUMMUS

Homemade hummus is a world of taste away from the supermarket stuff and luckily, with a wood-fired oven, the hardest part – cooking the chickpeas to a meltingly soft texture – can be done without the fuss and endless boiling needed on the hob to get them 'just right'.

140–150°C (275–300°F)
SERVES 4–6

150g (¾ cup) dried chickpeas (garbanzo beans)
150g (¾ cup) light tahini
2–3 cloves of garlic, crushed
juice of ½ a lemon, or to taste
about 6 tbsp ice-cold water
salt and freshly ground black pepper

Optional garnishes
a good drizzle of extra virgin olive oil
1 tbsp roughly chopped, fresh flat-leaf parsley or coriander (cilantro)
1 tbsp toasted pine nuts
2 tsp toasted cumin seeds
½ tsp smoked paprika

Before you go to bed, put the chickpeas into a large earthenware casserole and cover them well with at least triple their volume in cold water. Cover the pot with a tight-fitting lid or snugly tucked piece of foil and slide it into the oven. Leave undisturbed until morning.

In the morning, drain the chickpeas and tip them into a food processor while hot. Add the tahini, garlic and lemon juice and blitz to a coarse paste. With the motor running, begin to trickle in the cold water. It will emulsify the hummus to a smooth paste as the motor runs. I like hummus really smooth, so I keep the motor running for a good couple of minutes. Taste and add salt and freshly ground black pepper, and a squeeze more lemon if you like. Scoop into a bowl and allow to cool.

Chill until needed. Bring to room temperature before serving, topped with your favourite garnishes.

WHOLE ROAST ORANGES FOR A CREAMY MARMALADE-INSPIRED MOUSSE

The beginnings of this recipe couldn't have been lazier: I simply wrapped a couple of oranges in their own foil parcels and bunged them into the oven just before going to bed in a kind of chuck-it-in-and-see experiment. By the morning each orange had slumped and softened to a darkish mass, looking wholly uninspiring but smelling intensely, like a rich marmalade. This probably isn't a pudding your kids would relish, mine certainly didn't, but for the rest of us it was a luscious and creamy thing, with the sweet and bitter flavours that make marmalade so joyous. The cooked oranges freeze beautifully too, so you can save them for another time.

140–150°C (275–300°F)
SERVES 4–6

2 large oranges, skins scrubbed
    and left whole
200g (2 cups) caster (superfine)
    sugar
300ml (1¼ cups) double (heavy)
    cream
200g (1 cup) natural yoghurt
a few squares of dark chocolate,
    shaved into curls, to garnish

Wrap each orange in a generous sheet of foil so it is completely enclosed, and set them in a small roasting tin or baking tray. Once your oven is nice and cool (about 140–150°C/275–300°F), slide the tray in, shut the door and leave until morning – 8–10 hours will be fine.

In the morning, retrieve the oranges and unwrap them over the roasting tin so you don't lose any juices. Slice in half – they will be so soft you can do this with a table knife – and have a little fish around with a teaspoon to remove and discard any pips. Put the oranges (flesh, peel and juices) and sugar into a food processor and whizz to a really smooth purée. Alternatively, whizz them with a stick blender in a deep jug.

Hang a sieve over a bowl and pour in the orange mixture, pressing it through with a spoon and discarding any pithy bits. Set aside to cool completely. You can also chill the orange mix at this stage for a few days, or even freeze it until you feel like making fool.

Once the orange mixture is cool, put the cream into a separate mixing bowl. Whisk to soft billowy peaks, using a balloon or electric whisk, taking care not to overbeat. Fold in the yoghurt and the puréed orange mixture, leaving it a little bit swirly so you can see the orange layer. Spoon into a serving dish, or into individual dishes if you prefer. Chill in the fridge for about an hour, until set. It will sit happily in the fridge for 12 hours or so if you want to get ahead.

Just before serving, use a vegetable peeler to shave a few curls of dark chocolate over the top.

BEST EVER CHICKEN STOCK

This is the chicken stock recipe I've been happily making for years over a low heat on the hob but using the low, steady heat of the falling temperature of the wood-fired oven overnight has been something of a stock revelation – the resulting liquor is completely clear, deep and very flavourful. Leaving the onion skins on may feel odd but it gives a deep caramel colour to the stock.

140–180°C (275–350°F)
MAKES ABOUT 1.5–2 LITRES (6–8 CUPS) OF STOCK, WHICH CAN BE BAGGED INTO PORTIONS AND FROZEN

1 roast chicken carcass, broken into pieces no bigger than your fist
2 onions, unpeeled, roughly chopped
2 large carrots, unpeeled, roughly chopped
stalks from a large bunch of fresh parsley (save the leaves for another recipe), roughly chopped
3 bay leaves, fresh or dried
1 tsp black peppercorns
2 litres cold water

Simply put everything into a large stock pot, giving it a muddle around to mix and pressing everything as much as possible under the water. Cover with a tight-fitting lid or a snugly fitting layer of foil and set aside until you are ready to slide it into the oven.

Once you have finished cooking for the evening and you are ready to turn in to bed, simply slide the pan into the middle of the oven, close the door tight and leave well alone until the morning.

The stock will cook gently and very happily as you sleep – 7, 8, 9 hours, or even more if you are extremely lucky. In the morning, remove the pan and set aside to cool a little before pouring the warm stock through a colander hung over a large bowl. Allow it to go cold, then chill in the fridge until you are ready to use it. It will keep for 5 days or so chilled, or you can portion it up into freezer bags and freeze for another time.

OVERNIGHT DRIED TOMATOES

Another minimal-effort dish for overnight cooking, this is a great trick for adding bags of flavour to tomatoes that are not quite as sweet as you would like them to be.

130–150°C (265–300°F)

medium to large tomatoes, as many as you like, sliced in half

Spread the tomato halves out on a baking sheet, making sure there is a bit of room around them so that the heat can get all around. Use two baking sheets if you are drying plenty. Too tightly packed and they will cook down to a mush (albeit delicious) rather than dehydrate. No need to add any oil or seasonings, as you are just trying to dry them and concentrate the flavour. Slide into the oven.

In the morning, remove from the oven and set aside to get completely cold. Scoop them into a bowl, drizzle with a little extra virgin olive oil, season with a little salt and pepper and toss gently to coat. They will keep for a week, covered, in the fridge.

PORK RILLETTES WITH PICKLED BEETROOT

As an introduction to French charcuterie, pork rillettes are a complete doddle to make. Think of them like a cross between a pâté and pulled pork, very rich and flavoursome, very lovely spread on toast, and even better on the rye and caraway crackers on page 137. Pork belly always benefits from a low and slow approach to cooking, so it is suited to a long overnight braise in the wood oven.

130–150°C (265–300°F)
MAKES A LARGE JAR, 8 OR SO SERVINGS

For the rillettes

1.5kg (3lb 5oz) rind-on belly pork, boneless (about 1.1–1.2kg/2lb 6oz–2lb 10oz if it's rindless)
2 tsp salt
2 tsp black peppercorns, roughly crushed
1 tsp juniper berries, roughly crushed
½ a nutmeg, freshly grated (or 1 tsp ready-ground)
5 cloves of garlic, bruised and peeled
3 sprigs of fresh thyme
3 bay leaves
salt and freshly ground black pepper

For the beetroot pickles

2 small raw beetroots (beets)
4 tbsp white wine vinegar
2 tsp caster (superfine) sugar
1 tsp salt

For the parsley salsa

50g (1 cup) (½ a large bunch) fresh flat-leaf parsley
1 tbsp olive oil
1 tbsp white wine vinegar
1 clove of garlic, roughly chopped
1 tbsp capers
1 tbsp Dijon mustard

When you are ready to cook, you want the oven to have cooled to a gentle 130–150°C (265–300°F). See page 143 for tips on cooling a hot oven.

If your pork belly has rind on, use a really sharp knife to slice it off, peeling back the skin and using short slicing motions to pare away the skin. Discard the skin, or, even better, use it to make the pork scratchings on page 68.

Put the pork into a casserole dish – ideally you want it to fit in a snug single layer. Sprinkle over the salt, crushed peppercorns and juniper berries, and the nutmeg, rubbing it in all over. Tuck in the garlic, thyme and bay leaves. At this point you can refrigerate the pork for up to 24 hours if you want to get ahead, or you can carry on straight away and get it in the oven – because of the long slow overnight cook it doesn't really need marinating.

When you are ready to cook, pour about 500ml (2 cups) of cold water into the casserole dish, or enough to just cover the pork. Press a piece of baking paper down on to the pork to seal it in and cover with a tight-fitting lid or a snugly wrapped piece of foil. Slide into the oven and bake overnight.

In the morning, carefully lift the pork on to a roasting tray. Strain the juices though a fine sieve into a bowl and set aside to cool completely. You want to leave it so that the fat separates and rises to the surface.

Use forks to tease the meat into fine shreds, discarding any fatty membranes that lie between the layers of muscle. Once you have pulled all the pork apart, put the meat on a chopping board and chop roughly with a large knife until it is all cut into short strands. Pack into a terrine dish or a wide-necked jar, pressing down firmly. Use a tablespoon to skim off the fat from the bowl of juices, pouring it over the meat to completely cover it. Chill in the fridge for several hours before eating, ideally overnight. As the fat chills it will solidify and form an airtight seal protecting the meat, which will keep for a week as long as it's sealed. Once you break through the fat layer, eat within 3–5 days.

An hour or so before you want to serve your rillettes, make the beetroot pickle and parsley salsa. Peel and very thinly slice the beetroots and spread out on a flat dish. Sprinkle over the vinegar, sugar and salt and set aside for an hour, turning the slices over every once in a while. For the parsley salsa, put all the ingredients into a deep jug. Blitz to a purée with a stick blender and season to taste with salt and pepper.

Serve the rillettes with plenty of toast or crackers, with the pickled beetroot and parsley salsa on the side.

NEWSPAPER-BAKED RICH FRUIT CAKE

I have decades-old but vivid memories of my mum staying up half the night to bake the Christmas cake most years, always using her trusty Delia recipe. One of those big rich fruit cakes takes much time and gentle baking – too high a heat and the outside burns before the inside is ready. So I thought it might be the perfect thing for the dying heat of the wood-fired oven, and it works an absolute treat. A few things to note: do make sure your oven is not too hot, and make sure you insulate the tin with plenty of newspaper – a whole broadsheet is ideal – and set the tin on a baking rack to lift it above the direct heat. Begin this cake the day before you want to bake, to soak the fruit.

120–130°C (250–265°F)
MAKES ONE 23CM (9IN) CAKE

900g (6 cups) mixed dried fruit (raisins, sultanas, currants, dried cranberries, chopped dried dates, prunes, figs, apricots)

150g (1 cup) mixture of chopped glacé cherries and dried mixed peel, whatever ratio you prefer

100ml (⅓ cup) brandy, rum or whisky

250g (1½ cups) butter, softened to room temperature

250g (1½ cups) dark brown sugar

4 eggs

250g (2 cups) plain (all-purpose) flour

2 tsp baking powder

1 tbsp mixed spice

1 tbsp black treacle (molasses)

You also need a 23cm (9in) round springform tin, a whole fat newspaper, and string to tie it with.

Put the dried fruit, glacé cherries and chopped peel into a large mixing bowl and pour in the brandy, rum or whisky. Stir together well and leave for 12–24 hours, stirring once or twice, until the booze has soaked in.

Prepare the cake tin for baking by double-lining the base and sides with well-greased baking paper. Then take several sheets of newspaper and fold them in half lengthways, so you have a long band of paper that is approximately double the height of the tin. Repeat with more newspaper so you have enough to wrap around the outside of the tin. Tie the newspaper band securely around the tin with string – an extra pair of hands is useful here. Take another good few sheets of newspaper and use them to line a baking sheet. Set the tin on top. You will need more newspaper to cover the top of the tin as well.

Once the fruit has soaked, the tin is prepared and your oven has cooled to a lovely gentle 120–130°C (250–265°F), you are ready to make the cake. Depending on how insulated your oven is, it may take some considerable time to cool to this temperature (see page 143 for useful info on cooling the oven down), but don't be tempted to put the cake in when it's hotter than this, as you risk overcooking if it's left overnight.

Put the butter and sugar into a mixing bowl and beat together with an electric whisk for a few minutes, until really light and fluffy. Add the eggs, one at a time, beating really well after each addition. Once all the eggs are in, add the flour, baking powder and mixed spice and beat once more until smooth. Finally, add the soaked fruit and black treacle, and stir together until combined. Pour into the prepared tin and level with a table knife.

Take the final wad of newspaper and lay it over the top of the tin so it's covered. Rest the baking tray with the cake on it on a wire rack and slide the whole lot into the cool oven. Shut the door and leave overnight – it should cook very happily for 8 hours.

Remove from the oven, unwrap the newspaper and run a knife around the edge of the tin. Release the springform and slide on to a cooling rack to cool.

Once cold, wrap in baking paper and foil and store in an airtight tin until you want to eat it. It will keep very happily for 6 weeks or so. You can 'feed' the cake some extra booze if you want it super-rich: unwrap it at weekly intervals, stab a few holes all the way through with a skewer, and dribble over a spoonful of rum, brandy or whisky. Rewrap and put back in the tin.

OVERNIGHT PORRIDGE

This is an absolute breeze, and a great no-effort dish you can shove into the oven to squeeze out every last drop of energy from it. And what could be a nicer breakfast to wake up to on a chilly morning? The oven does need to be cool enough not to burn or dry out the dish – 120–130°C (250–265°F) is ideal – and as an extra precaution I always rest the porridge pot on a metal cooling rack so it's lifted above the base of the oven. Jumbo porridge oats are best, as they keep a bit of texture after the long, slow cooking. Don't worry about the liquid to oats ratio – overnight cooked dishes really need a lot of liquid to keep them well hydrated.

120–130°C (250–265°F)
SERVES A GENEROUS 4

150g (1 cup) jumbo porridge oats
600ml (2½ cups) cold water
400ml (1½ cups) milk

Simply put all the ingredients into a heavy-weight ceramic pot – a terracotta or earthenware casserole dish is perfect – and give them a quick stir. If you are cooking the porridge with any flavourings or fruit (see below for some ideas), this is the time to add them.

Tear off a sheet of baking paper and scrunch it up under a running tap. Shake off the excess water and unfold, tucking it over the top of the porridge. Cover the pot with a tight-fitting lid or a piece of foil.

When your oven is cool enough, slide a baking rack on to the coolest part of the oven floor. Sit the pot of porridge on the baking rack to lift it above the direct heat of the base. Shut the door and leave alone until the morning.

In the morning, 7 or 8 hours later, retrieve the porridge and serve with your toppings of choice.

WHAT TO FLAVOUR YOUR PORRIDGE WITH...

Before you cook:
• A handful of dried fruit – cranberries, raisins, chopped dates, prunes or apricots.
• A sprinkle of ground cinnamon or mixed spice.
• A chopped apple or two.

Once it's out of the oven:
• Sprinkle with brown sugar, or drizzle with golden syrup or honey.

ACKNOWLEDGEMENTS

Creating a book is always a collaboration of many minds and talents, and the biggest thank-you for this one goes to my lovely husband for helping me take my fire-obsession to the next level. Together we plotted, planned and built our wood-fired oven, a real labour of love that consumed far more weekends than is sensible. Thanks to my fab kids, Izaac and Eve, who tolerated the distraction admirably on the promise of (almost) limitless pizza!

A special mention should go to Terry Lyons, builder of wood-fired ovens, for spending the day with us to make sure our oven build was the best it possibly could be. Thanks, Terry.

Huge thanks to Sarah Lavelle for believing in my idea from the get-go, and to the creative team at Quadrille for making the thing of absolute beauty you hold in your hands. Photographer Jason Ingram has, once again, done me proud – big thanks, Jason, for your endless positivity as well as the stunning pictures. Massive thanks to my dear friend Jo Ingleby and to Danielle Coombs – both Bristol legends who cooked like total demons on the shoot days to help me create all the beautiful food you see in these pages.

Lastly, a cookbook is nothing without readers and enthusiastic cooks, so thanks to all of you out there who are using this book. I truly appreciate you all.

PUBLISHING DIRECTOR Sarah Lavelle
COPY EDITOR Annie Lee
DESIGN MANAGER Claire Rochford
SENIOR DESIGNER Katherine Keeble
COVER DESIGN Maeve Bargman
PHOTOGRAPHER Jason Ingram
FOOD STYLING Genevieve Taylor
PRODUCTION DIRECTOR Vincent Smith
PRODUCTION CONTROLLER Tom Moore

First published in 2018 by Quadrille,
an imprint of Hardie Grant Publishing

Quadrille
52–54 Southwark Street
London SE1 1UN
quadrille.com

Text © Genevieve Taylor 2018
Photography © Jason Ingram 2018
Design and layout © Quadrille Publishing Ltd 2018

All rights reserved. No part of this publication may be reproduced, stored in a retrieval system, or transmitted in any form or by any means, electronic, electrostatic, magnetic tape, mechanical, photocopying, recording, or otherwise, without prior permission in writing from the publisher.

The rights of Genevieve Taylor to be identified as the author of this work have been asserted by her in accordance with the Copyright, Design and Patents Act 1988.

Cataloguing-In-Publication Data: A catalogue record for this book is available from the British Library.

ISBN 978 1 78713 177 4

Reprinted in 2018, 2020 (twice),
2021, 2021
10 9 8 7 6
Printed in China

FSC
www.fsc.org
MIX
Paper from
responsible sources
FSC™ C020056